So, You Say I Ca

CW00470010

Frances Connelly:

The working-class woman's route to the vote

Sheena Macleod and Laura Linham

Published by One Million Project Publishing with NeoLeaf Press

ONE MILLION
PROJECT
PUBLISHING

First Print Edition 2018 OMP Publishing

ISBN--9781729179093

Printed in the UK

Cover Credits

The picture of Frances Connelly on the front cover is taken from a painting by Sally A. Barr.

Cover design by Susan K. Saltos.

One Million Project (OMP)

Supporting others through the power of words, art and music

***

After production costs, all proceeds from this book will go to supporting the One Million Project (OMP).

The One Million Project is a global group of authors, musicians and artists under the direction of Jason Greenfield. The aim is to raise money and awareness for Cancer Research UK and the homeless through the homeless charity EMMAUS.

OMP currently have four anthologies on sale.

All money raised from this book will be used to help with costs associated with publishing, promoting and marketing, OMP related books, music and artwork.

OMP website- http://www.theonemillionproject.com

INTRODUCTION

Forgotten Figures

On the 21st of November 1911, Frances Connelly made her way towards the entrance of the polling station at the Town Hall in Yeovil, England, to cast her vote. A policeman barred her way. Despite showing him her polling card, which proved she was entitled to vote in the South Somerset by-election that day, the policeman tried to stop her from entering the building.

Frances Connelly wasn't committing any crime. While women today are free to exercise their right to vote in Parliamentary elections, at this time all women in the UK were disenfranchised. Despite their promises, the Liberal Government was delaying discussing a Bill which would enable some women to vote in Parliamentary elections for the first time. But, fate had stepped in and afforded Frances Connelly a means of voting in the by-election that day and she intended to do so.

2018 marks the centenary of the 'Representation of the People Act 1918', which gave women over the age of thirty, who met property or educational requirements, the right to vote in Parliamentary elections in the UK. While this was a major step forward for women, some women were still not allowed to vote.

This victory for these women of means must have tasted bitter-sweet to the many working-class and younger women who had actively contributed to the wider suffrage cause but who were now left excluded by this Act. At this time, the UK was still deeply divided by social class. Although a huge battle had been won for women, for some women the fight for the right to vote in Parliamentary elections would continue for another ten years.

Less attention has been given to the role that working-class women played in women's suffrage compared to those from the upper classes. This book explores how one forgotten and disempowered figure, Frances Connelly, a widowed glove-maker from Yeovil, England, made history by voting in a Parliamentary election in 1911. Frances wasn't the only woman in the UK to have voted before the 1918 Act. Her story is placed within the context of the other women who voted in England, some of the contributions made by working-class women to women's suffrage, and the times in which these people lived.

Despite voting seven years before women were entitled to do so, Frances Connelly's name, along with many other working-class women, was sadly missing from the 2018 centenary celebrations. It is the intention of this book to put this matter right.

On the 24th of November 1911, the *Western Gazette* reported how — *"for the first time in the history of the constituency of South Somerset, a woman claimed and was allowed to exercise the Parliamentary franchise."*

With commemorations of the passing of the Representation of the People Act underway in 2018, it seems fitting to remember Frances Connelly. By casting her vote that day, she played a small but significant part in the larger fight to earn this right for all women. After Frances voted, local newspapers reported that her vote was counted along with the others.

Few national newspapers at this time picked up on Frances Connelly's remarkable story; that a woman had voted in a Parliamentary election while the law did not allow women to do so, and the world hadn't ended.

FRANCES CONNELLY—1911

A By-Election in Yeovil

As local men made their way to the polling station in Yeovil to cast their vote in the 1911, South Somerset by-election, a slow-moving suffragists' car toured the town displaying the banner 'Mothers Want Votes.'

Inside number 25 Salisbury Terrace, on Reckleford, forty-two-year-old Frances Connelly donned a warm coat with fur around the collar. She placed a large hat onto her dark pinned-up hair and walked out the front door.

1. Reckleford in Yeovil around 1890. Taken from Sherborne Road. Townsend runs off to the left and Reckleford runs off to the right.

For nineteen years, since the 1892 general election, the South Somerset constituency had been represented by Edward Strachey, a Liberal. His elevation to the peerage, as Baron Strachie, had led to the by-election (an election held in a single political constituency).

According to the local newspapers, there was a good chance that Edward Strachey could now be replaced by a Unionist (Conservative).

There was widespread unrest rumbling throughout the country, which had resulted in two general elections being called by the Liberal Government the previous year, one in January and then another in December 1910. At the root of the problem was the Liberal Government's attempt to rush through their social reforms and their Bill to raise taxes to fund these reforms. These changes affected Frances as much as anyone else.

While the Government's plan seemed worthy enough, to eradicate poverty, the means they had chosen to achieve this was the cause for much concern. These changes all seemed too much too quickly.

And, despite earlier promises, the Liberal Government was also now dragging its heels with regard to passing an Act which would give wealthy or university educated women the right to vote in Parliamentary elections. But, Frances wasn't wealthy or university educated. Even if this Act had been passed, she still wouldn't have been legally entitled to vote in the by-election being held that day. The irony of her situation wouldn't have been lost on her.

FRANCES CONNELLY- 1866-1881

Growing Up in Yeovil

Frances was born in Yeovil in 1866, as Frances Parker. She was the fourth of five children of James Parker, and his wife, Louisa Hayward, who had married in December 1851. James worked as a leather dresser in the gloving industry; preparing the leather for use. He was most likely born in Rotten Row in Yeovil.

Although it's not a particularly appealing street name, Rotten Row isn't an uncommon address and there were many roads with the same name throughout the UK. Amongst other places, there were Rotten Rows in Manchester and London — so called because horses were paraded there, especially at the time of fairs.

It's believed that Rotten Row in Yeovil was named after the famous broad track of the same name in Hyde Park, London, which is still reserved for the exercise of horses. For Yeovil, the name Rotten Row first appears in the Register of Electors and in the 1841 Census, but in the late 1800's, it was renamed as Market Street — which still stands today.

2. Houses in Market Street, Yeovil 1956

James's father, Nathanial Parker, was married to Jane Parker. Nathanial worked as a rope spinner; minding frames on which rope was spun. The couple lived in the small village of Misterton, not far from Crewkerne (about nine miles from Yeovil).

Frances's mother, Louisa, was born in 1829. By the age of twelve, Louisa was already working as a glove maker. Her father, John Hayward (an agricultural labourer) and his wife, Jean, lived in Wellington Street in Yeovil. Almost all the families in this street worked in the gloving industry, many starting much younger than Louisa.

Frances first appears in official papers in the 1871 census, when she was five years old. She was living at 32 Vicarage Street in Yeovil, with her forty-three-year-old father, forty-two-year-old mother and siblings—William (born 1855), Louisa (born 1858), Anne (born 1861), Parthena (born 1863) and Alice (born 1869).

The family shared their home with a lodger by the name of Mary Dowding, who was listed as a governess. It was not uncommon at this time to take in a rent-paying lodger.

3.   Vicarage Street, Yeovil. Circa 1920

It wasn't until the 11th of November 1874 that Frances was christened, along with a number of her siblings, with the registry in the Yeovil parish files marking her as Fanny Connelly, aged eight.

Page 142 of the baptism register, 1874, showing records for Frances (Fanny), Parthena and Alice Parker.

Almost all of France's immediate family worked in the gloving trade.

FRANCES CONNELLY 1881-1888

Working years

By 1881, Frances's family had moved from 32 to 13 Vicarage Street and the then sixteen-year-old Frances (still recorded as Fanny) was working.

By this time in Frances's life, the family had been joined by a two-year-old granddaughter, Florence Ophelia Parker. Florence was possibly the child of Frances's sister, Louisa Parker, who was twenty-two-years-old and married to Albert Benjamin Day, a twenty-year-old railway engine cleaner.

Louisa and Albert married in 1880 and went on to have ten children, eight of whom were noted in the 1911 census as working in the gloving industry in Yeovil. There is no further mention of Florence (above). Their children are listed as—Rose, Percy, Louie, Alice, William, Walter, Lily, Elsie, Bertie and Albert. The census had the family living at 15 Salisbury Terrace in Yeovil and Albert is listed as a railway engine driver.

Frances started work as a glover. From as early as the 1700's, the glove-making trade provided the main source of employment in Somerset and was Yeovil's main source of manufacture. The industry flourished in Yeovil and became of such significance that the town's Football Club is nicknamed 'The Glovers'.

Perhaps it is no surprise that like most other members of her family, and indeed, most other families in Yeovil, Frances entered the gloving trade. The industry provided work in three different but related trades: skinners, tanners, and glovers.

For more information on the gloving industry in Yeovil see Bob Osborn's A-to-Z of Yeovil. http://www.yeovilhistory.info/glove-process.htm.

Frances most likely sewed gloves using a sewing machine, which was used at the time, either working in a factory or from home.

4.   Picture of a sewing room at Giles & Co Clothier in the 1930's.

It is difficult to identify which glove manufacturers Frances and her family worked for. By 1840 there were thirty-six listed in trade directories for Yeovil and by the 1890's this had grown rapidly. By the early 1900's, about seventy to eighty percent of the town's population was involved in the leather, gloving and associated industries.

A man might be a glove cutter or leather dresser while his sons were apprenticed at the age of fourteen, frequently in the same trade as their father. Even in the 1920's the hours were long, with women often working from 5 am to 8 pm, with a one hour break in between. The gloving trade relied heavily on women. Married women and their daughters usually sewed gloves, many working part-time, in what was effectively a cottage industry. Girls started sewing from a young age and were often employed as early as seven-years-old to 'tie off' threads.

5. Glove maker, circa 1935

Manufacturers were represented by intermediaries, known as 'bagwomen'. These bagwomen supplied the raw materials to the home-working seamstresses, who were paid for every dozen pairs of gloves they completed.

The work was hard and the hours long, often for low wages. A series of labour law Acts had been passed by Parliament throughout the 1800's, to reform working conditions. According to an article by a school manager published in *Women's Franchise* in 1909, the Sweating Commission (in reference to the Factory Commission's enquiries), which urged reform on the working conditions of women at this time, had no impact because women couldn't enforce legislation.

As many women, and men, in the gloving industry worked in sweatshop conditions (long hours and low wages), mortality was also above average for the time. Working close together in confined spaces with poor ventilation meant that diseases spread quickly. Tuberculosis (TB) was prevalent. Like many other people, Frances Connelly had TB. And it is likely that she wouldn't have been the only member of her family to have this.

The Liberal Government had good reason to be concerned about the health of the nation. In 1900, about a third of the population lived in poverty and squalor. With harsh working conditions and low wages, the stability of the workforce was threatened, and concern grew amongst the upper-classes that the workers would revolt.

6. Workmen Leaving Platt's Works, (suppliers of spinning and weaving machinery) Oldham 20th August 1900

Many people feared the workhouse— where families were separated and conditions were harsh.

7. Dinner time in St Pancras Workhouse, London. 1911

Sixty percent of working class men at this time were not fit for military service. Overcrowding was rife, adding to the spread of disease. Lack of medical care led to many deaths from TB alone.

In the early 1800's, around one in four deaths in England was due to consumption (the old name for TB). TB continued to be a major cause of death amongst the working-classes until the 1940's, when the BCG vaccine received medical acceptance in the UK. In 1943, streptomycin also became available—this was the first antibiotic that was effective against TB. But, for Frances and many others before this time, there would have been little or no treatment available.

The Liberal Government had great hopes to implement their social reforms to help reduce poverty and improve the health of the workforce. In 1911, their means of doing so was causing great concern for the people of Yeovil.

FRANCES CONNELLY -1911

An Out for Out-workers

Of particular concern to Frances Connelly as she made her way to the Town Hall to cast her vote in the 1911 South Somerset by-election was the recent talk by the Liberal Government, reported in the local newspapers, about how their new National Insurance Bill (to provide sickness benefit to workers) would apply to out-workers.

8. Cover from a leaflet published by the Publication Department of the Liberal Party in 1911 promoting the future National Insurance Act.

Out-workers, like Frances and many other women in Yeovil, worked from home, often getting their raw materials from a range of different companies.

Two separate deputations, chiefly of glove makers from Yeovil, had travelled to London to put their case to a representative of the Chancellor of the Exchequer, asking for out-workers to be exempted from the National Insurance Bill. If employers had to pay a weekly 3 pence National Insurance contribution for each worker, as the Liberals were proposing, then many people could find themselves out of work. And, each worker was expected to contribute another 4 pence per week from their pay.

The issue of out-workers was of huge concern to the gloving industry in Yeovil. The profit from employing an outworker was already so small that employers were concerned it would be further reduced by the contributions they would have to pay for each of their out-workers. As a large number of people in the area earned their living in this way, the South Somerset by-election in 1911 was fought mainly on the exclusion, or not, of the out-workers from the Act.

And it wasn't just in Yeovil that workers were concerned about this. The boot-workers in Bristol had also petitioned Parliament.

The Unionists claimed to be on the side of the out-worker. The points raised by the deputation from Yeovil had been discussed within the House of Commons. And now, there was talk that the Liberal Government was considering exempting only married women out-workers. But, Frances was a widow.

Her concern likely grew, along with many others, that firms would now only employ married women for whom they didn't have to pay a National Insurance contribution. Coming from a family of glove-makers in Yeovil, in which many women, including Frances, were widowed or unmarried out-workers, she would have felt a need to do something about this.

And she did.

After leaving her home, Frances made her way towards Yeovil Town Hall. Her name was on the electoral register, entitling her to cast her vote in the by-election.

It is unclear whether she made the journey there alone. It seems likely, given the resulting newspaper report, in which there was no mention of anyone else, that Frances made her way unaccompanied to the polling station.

Frances had given the situation much thought beforehand. She knew which political party she would support and where and when she had to attend to do so. As a widow, she paid her own rent and rates, and now she intended to have her say about the MP who would represent her in Parliament.

No one knows for sure how Frances felt as she walked to the Town Hall, or how much courage it took for this forty-two-year-old widow to hold her head up and walk into the polling station with the full intention of casting her vote. Frances' face in the picture posted by the local newspaper afterwards suggests that she was proud and perhaps a little amused by the whole incident.

FRANCES CONNELLY—1888

Marriage and Children

Although Frances had grown up in Yeovil, she had spent many years living in London. On the 18th of March 1888, she was married in Hanover Church, the Parish Church in Middlesex. At the age of twenty-two, she wed twenty-five-year-old, Edward Connelly, a barman who lived in London. There was no record found of how Frances met her husband.

The two witnesses at the wedding are recorded as Walter (possibly Overall) and Rebecca (possibly Fryer).

Frances and Edward Connelly's Marriage Certificate 1888.

Thus, in 1888, Frances Parker became Frances Connelly.

Edward's father, also Edward, was an engineer. It's likely that Edward senior was born in 1832 in Scotland, where his family moved to from Ireland around 1830. He married Elizabeth (born 1831) and they lived in Middlesex. Edward's mother possibly came from Lambeth, London, where Edward was born in 1863.

Edward had four siblings, Ellen (born in 1859), Charles (born in 1861), Lydia (born in 1868) and Walter (born in 1870).

By the time Edward was seventeen, his father was fifty and unemployed. Edward junior had started working in a foundry, Charles had left home and Walter was working as a draper's assistant.

In 1891, three years after they had married, Frances and Edward were living in three rooms at 18 Esmerelda Road in Bermondsey in the London Borough of Southwark. Edward was working as a labourer, and the couple had a growing family; they had been joined by two sons, William and Walter.

By 1901, Frances was living at 99 Arlington Street, St James's, London. Edward was working as a 'potman' (barman), and the couple have another child, Edward. Frances was registered on the 1901 census form as Fanny Connelly.

According to the 1911 census, the year Frances voted, she was back living in Yeovil, at 25 Salisbury Terrace. She was forty-two-years-old and describing herself as the head of the household.

9. Postcard taken in the 1930's, of a house in Salisbury Terrace. (The houses were built by William Tucker, a glove manufacturer as homes for glove workers.)

Frances's oldest sons, William and Walter, are living at home with her and working in the leather industry. Her youngest son, Edward, was down as a scholar, and Frances had taken on a boarder by the name of Charles Page, a general labourer.

It is not clear when Frances's husband, Edward, died. Searches of London and Yeovil proved inconclusive. Frances and Edward aren't listed again as living together after the 1901 census. After Frances voted in 1911, one of the newspaper reports stated that she was a widow. The most likely conclusion is that after her husband died, sometime between 1901 and 1911, Frances and their three sons returned to Yeovil.

As a widow, Frances was now head of the household. No doubt this had contributed to her having been sent the polling card in error.

FRANCES CONNELLY-1911

Yeovil's First Woman Voter

Given that no women at this time had a legal right to vote in Parliamentary elections, it must have been daunting for Frances Connelly to enter the male domain of the polling station and assert her right to be there.

Now, as she stood outside the Town Hall with a policeman barring her way, Frances was faced with one of two options—turn around and go home or enter the polling station and cast her vote.

According to a report the next day in the *Daily Telegraph & Courier (London)* Frances demanded to be admitted. She had accidentally been sent the polling card when it was wrongly assumed that she was a man because her first name had been misspelt as Francis. Through a clerical error her name was recorded on the electoral register as Francis Connelly.

Within each polling district in the UK, a list of the names and addresses of people with the right to vote in Parliamentary elections is compiled annually. Only those included on this electoral register can vote.

In 1911, registers were compiled at a local level, with local polling districts being combined to form Parliamentary constituencies. Revising Barristers then held courts to revise the lists of voters within each constituency. The barrister reviewed statements from each of the officials who had drawn up the lists, in order to produce the final list of qualified electors.

For some reason, the clerical error leading to Frances Connelly's name being listed on the 1911 electoral register was not picked up.

The electoral register containing Frances Connelly's name.
She is listed as number 514 - Connelly, Francis - 25 Reckleford – Dwelling house.

Did Frances reveal this error to anyone at the time? Did she confide in her family, her fellow workers or friends and discuss what she should do? If she did, one can only imagine the varying reactions and advice she received. Or, did she remain silent about the error that had resulted in her now possessing the means to cast her vote in the by-election? It is likely that Frances kept this relatively quiet to avoid early detection and correction of the mistake.

What is evident is that, by not reporting the error or returning the polling card, Frances had kept the option open to cast her vote.

FRANCES CONNELLY-1911

A Yes for Yeovil

When Frances entered the polling station at the Town Hall, she was stopped again, this time by one of the presiding officials. The official refused to give her a ballot paper and challenged her as to her reasons for being there.

Imagine his bewildered surprise and resulting confusion when she informed him that her name was on the electoral register, that she carried a polling card made out in her name and that she intended to vote.

Having never experienced a woman turning up to vote in a Parliamentary election before, and knowing that the law entitled only some property owning or property renting men to do so, the presiding officials in Yeovil were unsure what to do.

They duly informed the chief Unionist agent (Conservative), Mr Harold Fletcher.

Mr Fletcher spoke at some length with Frances Connelly. He then argued her case with the barrister of the Western Circuit, Mr Snell, who happened to be assisting in the Committee-room at the time. (Circuit barristers provided advice on points of law which arose before, during and after elections).

After debating the issue together, Mr Fletcher and Mr Snell approached the presiding officer, Mr Henley, and queried with him Frances Connelly's right to vote. As presiding officer, Mr Henley was responsible for the conduct of the ballot in the polling station that day.

While these men had questioned her and debated her right to be there, Frances showed great courage and determination. She stood fast when approached and questioned by the officials. She remained firm while questioned, and waited under the scrutiny of other male voters while Mr Fletcher debated her issue with the presiding officer. Frances hadn't been intimidated by arguments to leave and was perhaps unsurprised when she was challenged and had been prepared for this.

After deliberating, Mr Henley finally agreed that he had no choice but to let Frances Connelly vote. Her name was on the electoral register and she met all the requirements to be allowed to vote in the South Somerset by-election.

The rules didn't actually say the voter had to be a man. The rules simply stated that it had to be a person listed on the electoral register and that they had not already voted in the election.

Frances may have experienced a sense of satisfaction when she was informed that she could indeed vote and, moreover, that her vote would be counted along with all the others.

Now free to place her vote, Frances put a cross alongside the name of Mr Aubrey Herbert, the Conservative (Unionist) candidate. Also standing was the Liberal candidate, Mr Henry Vivian.

In placing her vote that day, Frances Connelly secured her place in history. According to a report in the *Birmingham Daily Gazette* the following day, after entering her cross, Frances 'retired proudly.'

As she made her way out of the Town Hall, were the suffragists demonstrating outside and calling for votes for women aware of the unprecedented actions that had taken place inside? It would be surprising if they hadn't been. Great confusion had taken place both outside and inside the Town Hall and news of Frances Connelly's vote would have travelled fast.

There is mention in *The Daily Telegraph & Courier (London)* the next day, but not in other reports, that Frances Connelly had been accompanied inside by a suffragist who was 'much elated' when Frances was allowed to vote.

Perhaps women's suffrage campaigners were made aware that Frances Connelly had cast her vote that day. And, perhaps they acknowledged the impact of the landmark action that this working-class woman had made towards women's suffrage, not just in Yeovil but throughout the UK.

The following day, newspaper reports described how Frances Connelly attended the polling station at the Town Hall to make her mark in the 1911 South Somerset by-election.

Part of the report from the *Western Gazette*, on the 24th of November 1911 issue reads:-

South Somerset Election
Woman Votes at Yeovil

'The election will be remembered for the first time in the history of the constituency a woman claimed - and was allowed to exercise the Parliamentary franchise. At the very moment a Suffragists' car was touring Yeovil displaying to amused crowd the legend "Mothers want votes," the lady was putting her cross against the name of Hon. Aubrey Herbert—at least she was supposed to be on the Unionist side—at the Town Hall.'

Photograph of Frances Connelly appearing alongside the article in the *Western Gazette* on the 24th of November, 1911

The above article also featured in the *Taunton Courier and Western Advertiser* on the 29th of November. The newspaper report ends by confirming—*'What is more her vote was recorded in the ordinary way- not upon a tendered paper-and was counted with the others.'*

A tendered ballot paper is used where the presiding officer is uncertain if the person presenting to vote is the person on the electoral register, or where someone has already voted using the voter's name and number. The tendered ballot paper is a different colour from the other papers, usually pink. Instead of being put into the ballot box, the tendered paper is handed to the presiding officer who adds the name of the voter and their number and sets the tendered ballot paper aside in an official envelope. The voter's electoral number and name are then recorded on a list of tendered votes.

Rather than dealing with disputes in the polling station and holding up other voters who are waiting, tendered papers are given out and issues are considered once polling is finished. Unless the returning officer has reason to believe the tendered vote is unlawful, tendered votes would be counted.

The above newspaper reports confirm that Frances Connelly placed her vote in the ballot box.

FRANCES CONNELLY—1911

Frances's Vote in Context

In the polling station, Frances Connelly had put a cross against the name of the Conservative candidate (Unionist), Mr Aubrey Herbert, who beat the Liberal candidate, Mr Henry Vivian. At this time, the Prime Minister was Herbert Henry Asquith, a Liberal who was regarded as unsympathetic to women's suffrage.

10,546 electors had been entered onto the register for the by-election, and 92% voted.

It was thought by many at this time that women had no interest, or place, in politics. However, suffragette support for the Unionists was reported in the *Western Gazette*, 14th July, 1911, edition. And, Frances Connelly, an unsupported working-class woman also knew who she wanted to represent her when she cast her vote.

The Unionists had fought the campaign on the basis of supporting out-workers. An article on the by-election results featured in the *Birmingham Daily Gazette*, 22nd November 1911, reported:

'The only woman in South Somerset who has a vote showed today what she thought of Mr Lloyd George and his out-workers amendment to the Insurance Bill. Her name is Frances Connelly,

and by the irony of fate she is a widow. One of those who are not exempted from the proposed benefits of the Bill.'

When the result of the by-election was announced outside Yeovil Town Hall, around noon the next day, loud cheers erupted from the huge crowd who had gathered there. The Liberal belief that the Unionists couldn't win was rudely shaken and called into question the Government's plans for social reform.

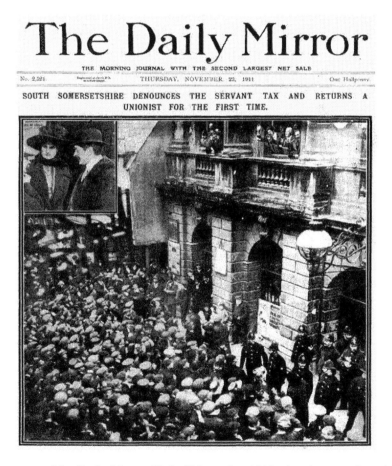

Front page of the *Daily Mirror*, 23rd of November 1911, showing crowds waiting for the election result outside Yeovil Town Hall. The small photograph shows Mr and Mrs Herbert.

A section from the accompanying report reads:

"*A Liberal stronghold, South Somerset has been captured by the Unionists. The campaign centred almost entirely around the Insurance Bill, and the electors have shown their dislike of that measure by returning the Hon. Aubrey Herbert by a majority of 148 over Mr Henry Vivian.*"

The Conservative Party was one of the two main political parties in the UK at this time, along with the Liberal Party.

10. Henry Herbert Asquith. Unknown date.

Asquith, pictured above, was Prime Minister from 1908. By 1916, however, the Conservatives became dissatisfied with his and the Liberal Government's handling of the First World War. Lloyd George had been pushing without success for a small war committee to be set up to provide more effective control of the war. In December 1916, Asquith resigned as Prime Minister.

The Conservatives formed a new coalition with some Liberals, under the leadership of David Lloyd George, a Liberal. Henry Herbert Asquith and the remainder of the Liberals moved into opposition.

David Lloyd George claimed to be pro women's suffrage.

THE PROOFS OF BETRAYAL

Suffrage refers to the right to vote in political elections. But voting was only a part of the fight for women's rights that occurred during the late 19th and early 20th centuries. Women's campaigns for equality with men extended to issues such as divorce, ownership of property, education and employment. That this basic right to equality was being denied to them incensed many women – and some men.

Women at this time played no acknowledged part in politics, and, according to Queen Victoria during her reign (1837-1901), this was as it should be. A woman's place, many still believed, was in the home. This continued to be said while many thousands of women throughout the country laboured in factories, many of them no more than sweatshops—for long hours and with low pay.

But it wasn't just in politics or work that women's rights were being denied to them. At this time women had few rights at all. It was much harder for a woman to divorce her husband than it was for him to divorce her. And, following a divorce, women had no right to keep their own property.

Women couldn't stand for Parliament and had many other restrictions imposed upon them — disobedient or transgressing wives could find themselves admitted to an insane asylum, as could a young woman who had a child out of wedlock. It wasn't until the Matrimonial Causes Act of 1937 was passed in the UK that a woman had the same right to divorce her husband as he had to divorce her.

Beginning in the 17th century, selling a wife at public auction was not uncommon as a means of divorce for the lower classes in England. During the sale, the woman was often paraded with a halter around her neck or a rope around her waist. The practice continued into the early 1900's, but by this time it had become a part of local custom.

Although it was demeaning, wife selling served a function. Unable to obtain a divorce through any legal or religious means, the sale of a wife was often carried out through mutual agreement or at the instigation of the woman. The sale was used as a means of dissolving the marriage.

11. Painting 'Selling a Wife'- Thomas Rowlandson. Wife being sold at market. 1812-14.

Where a woman wanted to remarry, her intended would be the one to buy her. The sale released the husband from any matrimonial responsibilities to the woman, including any financial responsibility.

Until 1918, women in the UK were unable to vote in Parliamentary elections. As such, they had little opportunity to influence the laws of the land, many of which worked against them or maintained their unequal status in relation to men both in the workplace and in society in general.

Although women's groups had been campaigning for the right to vote in Parliamentary elections from the early 1800's, it wasn't until 1867—with the formation of the National Society for Women's Suffrage (NSWS) by Lydia Becker—that suffrage became a national movement.

Branches had already formed, in London, Manchester and Edinburgh. These were soon followed with branches in the other large cities in England.

Thirty years later, in 1897, the National Union of Women's Suffrage Societies (NUWSS) was founded by Millicent Fawcett. These suffragists used peaceful methods of protest, such as lobbying.

In 1903, the Women's Social and Political Union (WSPU) was founded by Emmeline Pankhurst, and more militant campaigning commenced — including unlawful acts to attract attention and gain publicity. The 'suffragettes' had arrived. Many supporters of the WSPU were working-class women.

The distinction between suffragists and suffragettes went beyond their titles and methods of campaigning. Suffragists comprised a national society, suffragettes was a much smaller organisation. While suffragists allowed men to join their groups, the suffragettes did not. Because of their militant methods of campaigning, the suffragettes received more newspaper coverage, as was their intention.

The term suffragette was first used in 1906 by a Daily Mail journalist, Charles. E. Hands, as a derogatory term but the women adopted it and the term moved into common use.

Although their methods differed, both groups shared the same common goal — influencing public opinion and persuading people of importance that women should have the vote.

12. Members of the Women's Social and Political Union (WSPU) campaigning for women's suffrage.

There were many reasons why some women felt that they should have the right to vote in Parliamentary elections. Just as men did, they paid rates and taxes. Many women believed that this entitled them to an equal right to select the government they were paying for.

But, working women like Frances Connelly likely had additional reasons for wanting to have their say — in particular, to influence poor working conditions, low wages and the long hours that they worked.

13. Votes for Workers Poster. By W.F Winter.The Artists' Suffrage League, 1909.

Becoming a member of a women's suffrage organisation was not always an easy matter for working-class women. Like many other groups, money was required to finance these organisations.

The Conservative and Unionist Women's Franchise Association, for example, carried a membership registration fee of one shilling. This amount could have been difficult for low paid working women to spare. Even if these women could find the necessary fee, they had to pay a subscription of five shillings or more in order to find out when and where meetings would be held. Also, an optional annual contribution towards expenses was expected Membership badges cost one shilling. And, only those who subscribed a guinea or more were eligible for election to the women's council.

TAFFY WAS A WELSHMAN, TAFFY WAS A THIEF

Frances Connelly cast her vote in November 1911. That year, the UK had experienced the hottest summer on record. It was also the year of the coronation of the new King, George V, and Queen Mary, and the start of big changes in perceptions of leisure for the working-classes.

The *Woman's Weekly* magazine had been launched, advising women on how to run their homes and providing them with tips on how to feel good regardless of age. With cinemas opening, first in London and then throughout the rest of the country, a huge transformation in entertainment was also beginning to take place for the working classes.

14. . A few doors from where Frances lived in Yeovil, bunting and people out to celebrate the Coronation of King George V and Queen Mary,

There was also great unrest amongst the working classes throughout the UK, creating a crisis for the Liberal Government. Around one million workers throughout the country had taken strike action, including dockworkers, railwaymen and transport workers. But, it wasn't just men. The strikers included thousands of working women. In April, 15,000 women factory workers from twenty-three factories in Bermondsey, London, went on strike.

The years between 1906 and 1914 were marked by a period of social reform on a scale never seen before. To help relieve poverty, the Liberal Government pushed through legislation to introduce old age pensions, National Insurance (sickness benefit), insurance against unemployment, school meals and medical services for children, and some attempts were also made to improve working conditions and fix minimum wages.

These reforms were regarded with suspicion and sometimes even hostility by the working classes. Many could ill-afford to pay the proposed contributions out of their wages for services that they felt wouldn't directly benefit them.

The many restrictions attached to the new reforms gave workers good reason to believe this.

It wasn't compulsory for schools to provide free meals. Pensions would only be paid to those who had worked all their adult life. Few people thought they would live long enough to receive a pension at seventy (the average life expectancy at this time was around fifty-five). Low paid workers had to pay National Insurance Contributions out of their wages which they already struggled to live on. And, free medical care was only available to the wage-earner and not to their husband/wife or children.

Workers chanted "Taffy was a Welshman, Taffy was a thief" in reference to David Lloyd George, the Chancellor of the Exchequer, suggesting that he was stealing their wages. In reference to the contributions added to the worker's contribution by employers and the government, Lloyd George would respond back, 'Nine pence for four pence'.

The Liberal Government started introducing their welfare reforms immediately after winning the 1906 general election. And, the new social reforms needed to be funded. Lloyd George introduced the Finance Bill (also called The People's Budget) which taxed the rich in order to subsidise poor and ill workers. When the Finance Bill was passed by the House of Commons in 1909 but was blocked by the House of Lords, Asquith called a general election.

Unlike now, where elections are all held on a single day, general elections were held in constituencies over a number of days. The general election was held from the 15th of January to the 10th of February 1910. The Liberals were narrowly re-elected, and 'The People's Budget' was passed in April 1910.

In December 1910, a general election was held from the 3rd to the 19th of December. This was the second general election that year and the last to be held before the First World War. It was also the last election to be held over several days. After the election, the Liberal Party didn't have a majority in the House of Commons.

As Prime Minister, Asquith had the authority to approve new members of the Lords. As there was no limit as to the number of Lords at this time, Asquith said that if the Lords didn't pass the Parliament Act, he'd create enough new Liberal peers to outvote the ones who were blocking it. Asquith's Government secured the passage of the Parliament Act 1911, curtailing the powers of the House of Lords. This effectively abolished the power of the House of Lords to reject legislation or to amend it in a way unacceptable to the House of Commons.

The 'People's Budget', to finance reforms aimed at eliminating poverty, continued to be pushed through Parliament and was championed by two Liberals, David Lloyd George (Chancellor of the Exchequer) and Winston Churchill, (President of the Board of Trade).

15. David Lloyd George and Winston Churchill in 1907. Unknown.

David Lloyd George and Winston Churchill became firm allies, leading some Conservatives to refer to them as 'The Terrible Twins'.

CENSORING THE CENSUS

It was a census year in 1911, and in April the census was taken. The Government used that year's census to collect demographic and other information to help them gather figures to develop their policies for social reform.

For the first time, it was to be recorded how long women had been married, their disabilities, and how many children they had (including how many had died). The 'head of the family', usually a man, was now required to provide the government with a woman's personal details. The form had been extended to sixteen columns of personal information.

Many people, particularly the women whom new data was being gathered about for the first time, treated this with suspicion. The Government was now seen to be intruding into women's personal lives.

On the 2nd of April, enumerators would go out and collect this information from all households in the UK. The 'householder' was required to list these details for everyone who spent census night on their property.

Some women's suffrage groups urged their members to complete the 1911 census to assist the welfare reforms. But, after years of campaigning, many suffrage groups had grown frustrated by the

Liberal Government's continual broken promises regarding enfranchisement for a select group of women.

The Prime Minister, Henry Herbert Asquith, had further destroyed their hopes, when his Government rejected a People's Suffrage Bill in favour of a man only Bill, leaving many women's suffrage campaigners frustrated and furious. This, plus the additional information being gathered about women, turned the 1911 census into a battleground.

In protest against the Liberal Government's actions, and following the lead of the Women's Freedom League, suffrage leaders called on women to boycott the census. Women were urged to make sure that they were out of the house on census night or, if they had to be at home, to refuse to complete the form – this carried the risk of a £5 fine or even imprisonment.

While many reports of the time, and later, state that no one was charged or imprisoned for this, the *Western Gazette*, on Friday the 25th of August 1911, reported that Miss Mary Foster from Bournemouth appeared at court for refusing to fill in the 1911 census form. She was given the choice of paying a £5 fine or serving 14 days in prison. Mary Foster opted to go to prison and gave no other reason for refusing to fill in the form other than that she was a member of the Women's Freedom League.

Women used a variety of ways to protest against the new-style census. Some, like Miss Mary Foster, refused to provide the census information. Others spoiled the census form by writing comments on it or marking themselves as 'head of the household'. Many others stayed away from their homes that night, either in hiding or by gathering together somewhere or by moving around from place to place throughout the night so that they couldn't be recorded.

Newspaper reports of this time provide information about the actions that were carried out by women on census night.

In London — Suffragettes gathered for a midnight picnic on Wimbledon Common with banners proclaiming, 'If women don't count, neither shall they be counted'. Others met in Trafalgar Square where they spent the night.

Emily Wilding Davison (a suffragette who died two years later when she ran out in front of the King's horse at the Epsom Derby) successfully concealed herself in a crypt in the Houses of Parliament, so that she could claim to have resided there that night.

In Manchester—a large house packed with census evaders was renamed 'Census Lodge'.

16. Suffragettes gather in Manchester Census Lodge to boycott the 1911 Census.

Similar tales unfolded across the rest of the UK.

In Yeovil, Frances Connelly completed the census form, recording herself as 'head of the household'. Also listed are her three sons, William (twenty-two), Walter (twenty) and Edward (thirteen), plus a twenty-year-old male boarder, Charles Page.

While local papers reported anecdotal accounts of census boycotting in London and other areas throughout the UK, no mention was found of boycotting in Yeovil.

RAGES AND RIOTS

It's unclear whether Frances Connelly took an active part in the wider women's suffrage movement, but she would have been exposed to their campaigning. She spent years in London. The local newspapers, both in London and in Yeovil, reported almost daily at this time on actions for and against women's suffrage. And, members held public meetings up and down the country, including Yeovil and surrounding areas.

Pro women's suffrage campaigning first arrived in Yeovil in March 1883, when a public meeting was held in the Town Hall in support of the extension of the Parliamentary franchise to women householders and ratepayers. An ex-Mayor, Mr J. Bradford, presided, and there was a good attendance.

This meeting was reported in the *Western Gazette* on the 16th of March, under the heading 'Women's Suffrage.' The lengthy article includes the minutes from the meeting, which give a good account of the Yeovil members' reasons for supporting women's suffrage and makes for interesting reading.

A Mrs Clark pointed out that women required legislation to safeguard them as much as men did. She mentioned that until the Married Women's Property Act had come into force, a married woman was deprived of all her property. She thought it rather mild to say that a woman was 'deprived' of her possessions. *'But such were the contradictions of the law, especially when married women's possessions fell into the hands of the person who had promised to endow her with all that he possessed.'* Mrs Clark went on to talk about the unfairness of the present laws relating to the custody of children. She pointed out that reforms were needed in the divorce laws and that women should have a voice in the making of other laws which affected them.

She then spoke of questions about affairs of State—about peace and war, taxation, education, poor-law administration, and other matters. All of which she said, affected women just as much as they affected men.

A Mr Clinker thought it disgraceful that women and children weren't better protected from the outrageous assaults by some men who'd been brought before the police-courts. A magistrate would sentence a man who had stolen a few shillings' worth of property to a year's hard labour and the next day send another man who had kicked his wife half-to-death to prison for a week or two of hard labour. He pointed out that these cases turned up regularly in the town. While he believed in the protection of property, Mr Clinker asked, *'what was more important, the life and limb and honour of women and children, or a few pheasants?'*

At the end of the meeting, support for women's suffrage was carried, and a resolution proposed to send a petition to this effect to the House of Commons.

On Tuesday the 30th of November 1909, a suffragette meeting was held in Yeovil Town Hall. Although the event itself was free, admission was by ticket only. The meeting started out peacefully enough, but according to the *Western Gazette*, published three days later on the 3rd of December, it *'finished in a near riot'*. The paper reported on the turbulent scenes.

The main speaker was Evelina Haverfield, of the Women's Social and Political Union (WSPU).

17. Evelina Haverfield. Date unknown.

Evelina Haverfield was married to Major John Henry Balguy. On the 29th of June 1909, during a march to Parliament, which would later come to be referred to as the 'Bill of Rights March', she was arrested when, along with other WSPU members, she tried to enter the House of Commons to present the Prime Minister, Henry Herbert Asquith, with a petition for women's suffrage.

The event was reported in the *Western Gazette* on the 2nd of July, with the heading—'Suffragist Furies. Disgraceful Scenes. Martyrdom for two West Country Amazons.'

During the riots in November of the following year, Evelina Haverfield hit a policeman in the mouth. When charged, she was reported to have said, '*It was not hard enough. Next time I will bring a revolver.*'

As she addressed the audience at the 30th of November 1909 meeting in Yeovil, explaining that all the Women's Social and Political Union sought was equal voting rights with men, Evelina Haverfield battled to be heard against a roaring crowd outside and the noise from a chanting group of men at the back of the hall.

Then a mob, which had been gathering outside in the High Street, stormed the meeting. It was only after the police were called that order was restored and the speakers escorted away.

Over the following days, the events of the meeting were reported in newspapers throughout the country. The *Aberdeen Press and Journal* in Scotland reported, "*100 forced entry, hurling stones and other missiles at the speaker. Fighting broke out and the police were called.*"

Unsurprisingly, this first public meeting of the Women's Social and Political Union (WSPU) in Yeovil appears to have been their last. However, the following year Mildred Mansel set up a branch of the WSPU in Yeovil. She held the post of branch president and Evelina Haverfield held the post of honorary secretary.

In January 1912, a branch of the National Union of Women's Suffrage Societies (NUWSS—a suffragist organisation) was formed in Yeovil, with Miss Pocock as secretary and Mr Body as treasurer.

In 1913, a branch of the Conservative and Unionist Women's Suffrage Society (CUWSS) also formed in Yeovil.

So, by 1913 there were a number of suffragist and suffragette groups in Yeovil. And, a request was posted that year in the January edition of '*Votes for Women*', the Women's Social and Political Union (WSPU) newspaper, asking for any suffragists from Yeovil to contact a Mrs Bentinck in London.

Groups opposed to women's suffrage also formed. A meeting was arranged in January 1913 at the Digby Assembly Rooms in Sherborne, by the National League for Opposing Woman Suffrage.

AGAINST
WOMAN
SUFFRAGE.

PUBLIC MEETING

IN THE

ASSEMBLY ROOMS, SHERBORNE,

On THURSDAY, JANUARY 23rd,

AT EIGHT P.M.   DOORS OPEN AT 7.30.

SPEAKERS:

Mrs. GLADSTONE SOLOMON,

Mr. ALEXANDER MACONACHIE, M.A.

ADMISSION FREE.

THE NATIONAL LEAGUE FOR OPPOSING WOMAN
SUFFRAGE,
CAXTON HOUSE, WESTMINSTER, S.W.

Advert appearing in the *Western Gazette* on the 17th of January 1913.

The meeting was presided over by a local butcher and churchwarden, fifty-six-year-old Mark Parsons. The guest speaker was Alexander Maconachie who, when asked what he thought about force-feeding suffragettes in prison, replied that he, *"didn't think he would forcibly feed the suffragettes"*. Instead, he would put the food beside them and leave them to make their choice, and if they insisted on dying he would let them. He added that he had great faith in the odour of steak and onions at the right moment.

In 1914, two houses to the north of Yeovil were damaged by fire. Police suspected a WSPU member Hilda Burkitt, who was later tried for arson in Bath. No Yeovil suffragettes were thought to have been involved in this incident.

1914- A WORLD AT WAR

In August 1914, the Prime Minister, Henry Herbert Asquith, took the UK into the First World War. This would have had an immediate impact on Frances Connelly: thrusting her into the harsh realities of life during wartime. She had three grown sons; William, Walter and Edward who lived at home with her. By this time, Frances was forty-five and still living in Yeovil — the family has moved from 25 Salisbury Terrace to 1 Salisbury Terrace.

Reservists and territorials (non-professional soldiers who trained in their spare time) were called up and the first groups left Yeovil in the first week of August. The following day, a further one-hundred reserves signed up.

Frances's oldest son, William Edward Connelly, was among the first few hundred men from Yeovil to sign up to fight in the war. He joined the 5th Somerset Regiment (Reservists).

There is a mention in the *Western Chronicle* on Friday the 31st of August 1917, that Gunner William (W. E.) Connelly, 1 Salisbury Terrace, Yeovil had won a solid silver cigarette case in a machine gun team race. The report also mentions that William had seen action in France and had been transferred to the Machine Gun Corps.

18. Reservists marching to Yeovil train station – August 1914

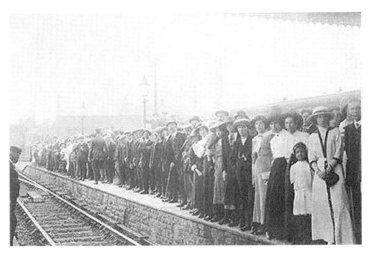

19. Yeovil Station. 1914 –Volunteers and their families

Frances's second son, Walter, also enlisted. Her youngest son, Edward, was sixteen at this time, and was too young to join up at the start of the war. There is a record of an Edward. Connelly, Private, in 1916. An article in the *Western Chronicle,* 11th of August 1916, reports an appeal against conscription, submitted from Yeovil to the Somerset Appeal Tribunal, by an Edward Connelly, aged eighteen. Edward asked to be allowed to remain in his present employment with Messrs. T. H. Swaffield as a motor engineer until his apprenticeship ended on his reaching nineteen. His appeal was dismissed.

Meantime, with the outbreak of war, militant suffragettes suspended their campaigns to help with the war efforts; although lobbying continued.

20. Women making shell cases in Reckleford, Yeovil. Circa 1915

By this time, it was increasingly clear that most of the key suffragette leaders had shifted away from demanding universal suffrage to fighting for the vote on 'the same terms as men'; that is, property renting or owning adults over the age of twenty-one. This caused a split within the suffragette ranks.

Now, it looked as if a women's suffrage Bill based on property, age and education requirements would be passed. And, the vote for many working-class and younger women would have to wait.

BITTER-SWEET VICTORY

The Representation of the People Act 1918 was passed by the wartime coalition government of Liberals and Conservatives, headed by David Lloyd George—a Liberal who had replaced Henry Herbert Asquith as Prime Minister. This Act entitled women over the age of thirty who met set property or educational requirements to vote in Parliamentary elections.

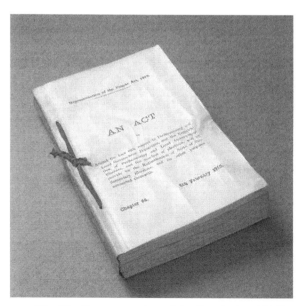

21. The 'Representation of the People Act 1918'

While the passage of the 1918 Act was a major step forward for women, it was a bitter-sweet victory for many of the working-class women who had fought so hard and for so long for women's suffrage. Despite their efforts, they were still not able to vote in Parliamentary elections, thereby limiting their ability to influence the Government to improve their working conditions and level of pay, which for many were extremely poor.

Although the Government had listened to some women's voices, they had not listened to them all. The fight for equality with men, and now also with some women who were better off than them, would continue for many working-class women.

The fight had to continue.

It took ten years.

WORKING-CLASS WOMEN AND WOMEN'S SUFFRAGE IN THE UK

The Representation of the People Act 1918 enabled some women over the age of thirty to vote in Parliamentary elections for the first time. But it wasn't just women's suffrage that had driven this change.

At this time, almost half the adult men in the UK weren't eligible to vote in Parliamentary elections. Not only were men required to own or rent property, they also had to be resident in the country for the year prior to the election. But, this meant that men serving abroad in the war lost their voting rights.

With a general election imminent, Parliament abolished the restrictions for men and extended the vote to all men over twenty-one and women over the age of thirty who met set property or educational criteria. The same year, the Parliament (Qualification of Women) Act, 1918 was passed, allowing women to become Members of Parliament (MPs) for the first time.

Although the Representation of the People Act 1918 proved a large step forward in women's suffrage it still excluded some women (and some men) from voting in Parliamentary elections.

Little is currently known about the part Frances played, if any, in the wider suffragist cause. She didn't leave behind a diary or other record of her life. Like most other working-class women at this time, her contributions to women's suffrage would only become known if they became newsworthy—mainly by holding a position in one of the main suffrage or union groups or by being arrested.

Women's suffrage is often presented as groups of wealthy, upper-class women fighting for the rights of all women. But, there were different factions. Some suffrage groups fought for the vote for all women. Other groups did not. Many believed that the vote should be given only to educated or property-owning women.

Thousands of working-class women contributed to women's suffrage in various ways. Like Frances Connelly, their stories are often less well known or publicised. Until more of these women are acknowledged their names will remain buried in the archives.

Dora Thewlis

22. Dora Thewlis. By Daily Mirror Photographer March 1907

In 1890, Dora Thewlis (Dorothy) was born in a Yorkshire mill town. She was the fifth of seven children of weavers. Like most other working-class girls in the area, she started work in a mill at the age of ten. At the age of sixteen, she joined the Women's Social and Political Union (WSPU) and campaigned for women's suffrage.

On March the 20th, 1907, she joined hundreds of Yorkshire and Lancashire women from the cotton and worsted mills, to march to the House of Commons — defended by more than 500 police — to make their discontent known. Many of the women were dressed in shawls and clogs and were members of the WSPU.

Dora was one of the seventy-five women arrested and taken to prison. The following day a photograph appeared on the front page of the Daily Mirror, of Dora being removed by police officers.

23. Front page of the *Daily Mirror*— March the 21st 1907

Dora Thewlis became known as 'The Baby Suffragette'— a young mill worker who wore clogs and a shawl. She became newsworthy, not so much because she was working-class, but because of her young age.

Lilian Lenton

24. Lilian Lenton (Circa 1914)

Lilian Lenton, a twenty-one-year-old dancer; was a member of the WSPU (Women's Social and Political Union). Born in Leicester in 1891, she was one of five children. Her mother was a housewife and her father a carpenter-joiner.

Lilian Lenton became one of the 'most wanted' suffragists in the UK, for fire-raising and other illegal acts, such as window breaking. It was common for suffragettes to use fictitious names to protect themselves and their families. Amongst other names, Lilian Lenton assumed the alias of Ida Inkley.

Militant suffragette action of setting fire to buildings, damaging property and attacking people caused widespread condemnation throughout the country. While some people applauded such action, many became fearful and many more were outraged. It was hard for some women to justify such behaviour and this caused a split amongst suffragettes, with splinter groups forming who advocated less militant action.

Throughout 1913, *The Gloucester Journal* ran a column called, 'The Militant Suffragists'–which reported on suffragette attacks and subsequent trials.

Force-feeding suffragettes who went on hunger strike became a widespread practice. Lilian Lenton was one of the many people who were force-fed in prison and then released under the Prisoners (Temporary Discharge for Ill-Health) Act 1913. Under this Act, women on hunger strike could be released from prison if they showed signs of becoming ill. Once recovered, the women could be returned to prison. On their release, many women went into hiding, and the Act became known as the 'Cat and Mouse' Act.

25. –– WSPU poster. May 1914- by David Allen &Sons, Harrow - London.

On Friday 27th June 1913, *'The Suffragette'* newspaper reported on the condition of women — arrested ten days before —who had gone on hunger strike and had been released under the Cat and Mouse Act. The women were reported to be in a weak state, some being accompanied by a nurse and conveyed by cab.

26. WSPU poster showing a suffragette being force-fed through a nasal tube. 1910. Author Alfred Pearce (1855–1933) *-nom de plume* "A Patriot"

In 1909, Mabel Capper, a member of the WSPU, was among the first women to suffer force-feeding while on hunger strike in prison and to describe the treatment she received while she was held at Winson Green Prison in Birmingham.

27. Mabel Capper outside Bow Street Court after her arrest in 1912.

She joined the WSPU in 1907 and worked as an Organiser for the Manchester branch. In one of the first accounts of force-feeding in prison, she described in a scrapbook the horrors inflicted upon her.

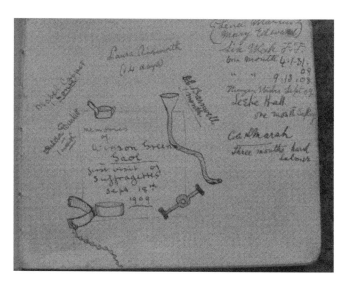

28. Mabel Capper's scrapbook showing the method used to force feed her.

The above drawings, taken from a page in Mabel Capper's scrapbook, show the manacles used to hold her legs and arms and the long tube which was inserted down her nose or throat. Her mouth was forced open with a metal clamp. The procedure wasn't only demeaning, it was dangerous.

Women started to report rectal and vaginal feeding — which makes little or no sense in terms of force-feeding. It would seem that this was through inserting suppositories. One woman, Fanny Parker, wrote about her experience of being force-fed through suppositories inserted into her rectum whilst she was retained in Perth Prison. Many women also reported being fed with tubes that had not been properly washed since their last use.

Lilian Lenton almost died through being force-fed in prison. She'd been tied into a chair, had her head dragged backwards by her hair and then had a tube forced through her nose. She developed pleurisy, suggesting that food or fluid had entered her lungs. She wasn't the only woman to have nearly died as a result of having been force-fed.

As news of the assault of these women began to spread, widespread condemnation surfaced. In a bid to draw attention to the issue, Emily Wilding Davison, who later died when she ran onto the racecourse during the 1913 Derby, threw herself from a prison window, which was eight feet from the ground. She was saved from death or serious injury when her fall was broken by wire mesh.

In a BBC interview, first broadcast in January 1960, Lilian Lenton describes how she escaped police surveillance while released under the Cat and Mouse Act. Despite her best efforts, and the efforts of others, when the 1918 Act was passed, Lilian Lenton still couldn't vote.

Hugh Franklin

It wasn't only women who were active in the women's suffrage movement or force-fed in prison. A few men were force-fed too. The first person to be released under the Cat and Mouse Act was a man.

Hugh Franklin was repeatedly force-fed while imprisoned. He was left so weak that he was released as soon as the Act came into force, making him the first person to be let out under the Act.

29. .Hugh Franklin 1911

The Home Secretary, Winston Churchill, was widely blamed for sanctioning the excessive force used by the police at the demonstration which took place on the 18th of November 1910 (Black Friday).

Hugh Franklin took part in this rally on Parliament. Angered by the brutality he witnessed towards protesters and by the harsh treatment of hunger strikers in prison, he later assaulted Winston Churchill with a dog whip. And on another occasion, he threw stones at Churchill's house.

On both of these occasions, Hugh Franklin was imprisoned. During these and other terms of imprisonment, he went on hunger strike and was repeatedly force-fed.

Constance Lytton

30. WSPU members 1911. Constance Lytton is in the foreground.

Constance Lytton, a daughter of an earl, believed that working-class women were treated more severely in prison than educated and upper-class women.

In 1909, she'd joined the Women's Social and Political Union. While in prison she'd never been assaulted or force-fed. The following year she attended a protest, disguised as a seamstress and using the name Jane Warton. After she was arrested and sentenced to prison, she went on hunger strike and was force-fed. On one occasion a doctor slapped her face.

The force-feeding of hunger-striking women and men was dangerous to their well-being. In some cases, it affected a person's long-term health.

Once her true identity was revealed, Constance Lytton was released. She published a book on her own and other suffragists' experiences in prison, entitled 'Prisons and Prisoners'.

Annie Kenney

31. Annie Kenney

Annie Kenney was born in the West Riding of Yorkshire, into a large working-class family. At the age of ten, she started working part-time in a cotton mill and began full-time work at thirteen as a weaver's assistant. Later, she became involved in trade-union activities.

At the age of twenty-six, she stopped working and moved in with the Pankhursts. The following year, 1906, she moved to London, where along with Minnie Baldock, she formed the first branch of the WPSU in Canning Town.

In June of that year, Annie Kenney was arrested when, along with others, she tried to obtain an audience with the Chancellor of the Exchequer, Asquith. Given the option of serving six weeks in prison or give up campaigning for a year, she chose prison, as did the others.

She was the organiser for the West of England branch of the WSPU, which included the South Somerset area where Frances Connelly lived. Annie Kenney died in 1953 at the age of 73.

Violet Ann Bland

32. Violet Ann Bland - circa 1912

Born in 1863, the oldest of nine children, Violet Ann Bland (Annie) worked as a kitchen maid in Shropshire. She later ran a hotel in Cirencester, and then bought property which she rented out. After moving to Bristol to open a country house hotel, she became active in the women's suffrage movement.

In 1910, Henry Herbert Asquith, Prime Minister, who was regarded as unsympathetic to women's suffrage, announced that if he was re-elected he would introduce a Conciliation Bill on women's suffrage—extending the right of property-owning women to vote in Parliamentary elections.

The Conciliation Bill was put before the House of Commons, in 1910. Although it passed its first and second readings, Asquith refused to give the Bill further Parliamentary time and announced a general election. A pattern of broken promises was now established.

The Women's Social and Political Union (WSPU) felt betrayed. They stepped up their militant campaigns and started a widespread attack on property and organized a protest march.

33. Leaflet distributed by the Women's Social and Political Union. 1910

34. WSPU members making banners. 1910.

On the 18th of November, 1910, Annie joined about three-hundred other women and some men as they marched to the Houses of Parliament. Many people today hear the term Black Friday referred to as a day for cheap retail deals. But, in 1910, the term was applied to this women's suffrage protest which turned into a scene of horror in which at least two suffragettes died and many more were injured. Annie was among those arrested.

35. Daily Mirror 19th of November 1910. Black Friday.

When the protesters tried to break through police lines, they were beaten and abused for many hours. Over a hundred people were arrested. The Home Secretary, Winston Churchill, was thought to have authorised the police to use force against the protesters. He then refused a public enquiry into the violence used by the police and male bystanders.

The following day, the front page of the Daily Mirror carried a harrowing picture of an attacked woman lying injured on the ground.

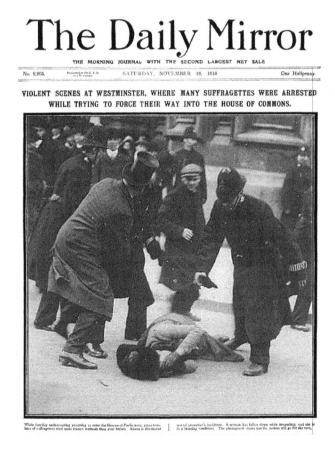

36. Front page of the *Daily Mirror*, 19th of November 1910, showing an attacked suffragette lying on the ground. Photograph by Victor Consolé.

The Parliamentary Franchise (Women) Bill was defeated again in 1911 and once again the following year. The suffragettes responded by upping their militant campaigns and started targeting the homes of Henry Herbert Asquith, Winston Churchill and David Lloyd George, amongst others.

In 1912, when suffragettes rampaged through London in protest, smashing windows and causing widespread damage, Annie Bland was again arrested. In court, she refused to promise to keep the peace and was sentenced to four months in prison.

Catherine Griffiths—The Last Suffragette

Born in 1885, Catherine Griffiths was the daughter of a Welsh miner. Originally from Glamorgan, Catherine Griffiths moved to London as a nurse and became active in the suffragette movement there.

A campaigner of Finsbury, she was a councillor there between 1937 and 1965, becoming mayor in 1960.

Catherine Griffiths died in 1988, at the age of 103, earning her the title of the last surviving suffragette.

WORKING-CLASS WOMEN INVOLVED IN DEPUTATIONS

In 1913, David Lloyd George (Chancellor of the Exchequer), and Sir Edward Grey (Foreign Secretary), despite refusing to meet with suffragette leaders, agreed to meet with a deputation of working women to hear what they had to say about women's suffrage.

Twenty women, including factory workers, fishwives, laundresses and weavers, met with them and put their case forward. The women spoke about low wages and how the vote for women might improve conditions for them.

In 1914, Henry Herbert Asquith (Prime Minister) met with a deputation of six working women from East London; Julia Scurr, Elsie Watkins, Jessie Payne, Mrs Savoy, Mrs Bird and Mrs Parsons.

Despite repeatedly refusing to meet with members of any organised suffrage movement, the Prime Minister listened to this group of working-class women as they explained how working women's livelihoods were at stake, and how their lack of a vote left them disempowered to do anything about this.

WOMEN VOTERS—THE FIRST SEEDS ARE SOWN

While Frances Connelly's vote in the South Somerset by-election caused surprise at the time, she wasn't the only woman to vote in a Parliamentary election in England before 1918.

Although women were excluded from voting before this, it is wrong to assume that no women actually did. There is evidence— mainly through newspaper archives—that many women voted in Parliamentary elections in the UK before the 1918 Act came into force.

Historically, restrictions on the franchise in the UK, based on property ownership, age and gender, were set more by tradition than by statute. In the thirteenth century, only men over the age of twenty-one could vote, and then only if they owned propertied land. Effectively, the property criteria excluded six out of seven men from voting and left the political power of the country very much in the hands of the landed gentry.

Until the 19th century, there was no electoral register. People who held properties in different geographical areas could vote multiple times (plural voting). In 1832, a major reform was carried out (The First Reform Act). For the first time, overseers from each parish had to draw up a register of all 'persons' entitled to vote and to publish this annually. Voting rights were extended to male householders who paid more than £10 annually in rent. Shopkeepers were also entitled to vote.

Until the 1832 Reform Act, women were not explicitly banned from voting. But, by using the term 'male persons' in the new Act for England and Wales voters were now considered to be men and women were excluded. At the same time, a separate Scottish Reform Act was introduced.

In 1832, Mr Henry Hunt, MP for Preston, presented the first petition to Parliament from a woman asking for the vote. Mary Smith was from Stanmore in Yorkshire. The petition stated that as Mary Smith paid taxes and was subject to the rule of the law just as men were, including capital punishment, she didn't see why she shouldn't vote. The petition was laughed out of the House of Commons. And, until 1867, any attempt to amend the 1832 Act was resisted in Parliament.

In 1866, the first mass petition was drawn up for women's suffrage and presented to Parliament by the Liberal MP, John Stuart Mill. And The Reform League, established in 1865 to press for manhood suffrage, became more active and held a number of demonstrations of many thousands of people in Manchester and other large areas.

In July 1866, a peaceful demonstration by men was organised to take place in Hyde Park, London, to protest against the failure of the Reform Bill. The Conservative Home Secretary, Spencer Horatio Walpole, banned the demonstration. When the demonstrators turned up anyway at Hyde Park, they found the gates chained and thousands of troops and policemen preventing them from entering. Over a thousand foot and mounted police guarded Marble Arch alone.

Following three days of rioting, the protesters discovered that the park railings were not secure. After much rocking back and forth, the railings gave way and thousands of demonstrators flooded into Hyde Park. The crowd was so large the Government did not order an attack.

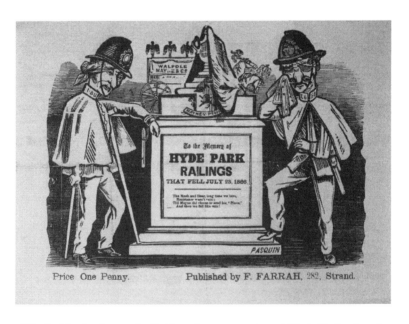

37. Satirical print on the Reform League protest at Hyde Park, showing a funeral being held for the railings.

Faced with the possibility of further revolt, the Government quickly introduced the Representation of the People Act, 1867 (the Second Reform Act). This Act extended the vote in England and

Wales to 'respectable' males over thirty who were small landowners, householders or lodgers in towns paying £10 or more a year in rent — prior to this Act only 1 in 7 men could vote. While the new Act effectively doubled the number of men eligible to vote, it still excluded the large majority of working-class men and all women.

The Representation of the People Act (Scotland) and the Representation of the People Act (Ireland) were introduced in 1868.

The Third Reform Act (The Representation of the People Act 1884) increased the UK electorate further—with even broader property and rental criteria for men—but still failed to make any changes for women.

From the 1832 Reform Act until the 1918 Act, all women were effectively excluded from voting in Parliamentary elections, through the use of the term 'male' persons in Reform Acts. Despite this, since the Second Reform Act was passed in 1867, a number of women slipped through the net. Many of these women succeeded in voting in Parliamentary elections.

A CONFUSION OF CHRISTIAN NAMES

In 1869, the Municipal Franchise Act was passed by Parliament, entitling unmarried rate paying women to vote in local elections. This meant that women could appear on municipal electoral registers.

By the early 1900's, 300,000 women could vote for town councils and 500,000 for county councils. As these women were unmarried or widowed, their names would appear as rate payers either for shops they owned or rented or as home owners (or renters).

The rate book or rate collectors' list was the principal source of drawing up the electoral register. And here is where the problem started, with women who had male sounding Christian names (like Frances and Lois) now being added onto the electoral register from the municipal register through clerical error.

The 1867 Manchester by-election

In November 1867, a widowed shopkeeper in her late sixties, Lilly Maxwell, was included on the voting register for the Parliamentary by-election in the Chorlton-upon-Medlock township of Manchester. Lilly's name (like Frances Connelly's later) had been placed on the register through clerical error.

The death of Edward James, a Liberal, had led to the by-election.

Lilly Maxwell turned up at Chorlton Town Hall and voted for Mr Jacob Bright, a Liberal, who won the Manchester seat. Jacob Bright was an active supporter of both women and men's suffrage.

38. Liberal Politician. Jacob Bright. 1899 or earlier.

That year, the 1867 Representation of the People Act (the Second Reform Act) had extended the right to vote to all property-owning men over the age of twenty-one — including lodgers who paid £10 or more a year in rent.

Although this Act was approved in August 1867, it specified that any by-elections held before the 1st of January 1869 would take place under the pre-1869 conditions — that is, under 'The first Reform Act- 1863' — which had extended the franchise to small landowners, tenant farmers, shopkeepers and all householders who paid a yearly rent of £10 or more and some lodgers.

The shop and house Lilly Maxwell rented in Manchester qualified her to vote under the old £10 borough franchise.

39. Lilly Maxwell. Circa 1867.

Lilly Maxwell was acknowledged as the first woman to vote after the 1832 Reform Act. Encouraged by Lilly Maxwell's vote in the 1867 Manchester by-election, and recognising a loophole in the law—which allowed property-owning women and shopkeepers to vote until January 1869, when the new Act came into force — Lydia Becker (a women's suffrage campaigner and founding editor of the *Women's Suffrage Journal*) urged women in the UK who possessed the required qualification to get their names on the register for the upcoming 1868 general election.

As a result, thousands of women got their names included on the voting register; most were removed by revising barristers. In Aberdeen, the assessor, John Milne, a suffragist, allowed over a thousand women's names onto the register, but these were removed by the Sheriff's Court — the principal civil and criminal court in Scotland.

Throughout the rest of the country, women's names were added and struck off, and the appeals against this started — *Liverpool Mercury* 17th September, 26th September and 10th November 1868.

In Leicester, Edith Gittens, President of the Leicester Women's Liberal Association appeared before the Revising Barrister to support the claims of eighteen women who wanted to be admitted to the list of Parliamentary electors. All of these women were refused.

Across Manchester, around 6,000 claims by women were lodged in the registration courts in September 1868. But these claims, along with the claims of thousands of other women across England, were rejected by the Revising Barristers.

The appeals against those whose names had been removed, however, finally proved disastrous for women's suffrage. In November, judges in England finally ruled that the 1867 Reform Act did not apply to women. The women's votes were declared illegal by the Court of Common Pleas, and the loophole was plugged.

A similar story occurred in Scotland. Browne v Ingram was heard on the 30th of October, Mary Browne lost — the judges ruled that her name had properly been struck off the electoral register.

Although many wondered if these decisions were supported by statute or judge-made law, the decisions stood. But, many women continued to try to get their names on the electoral register — some misspelling their name in the hope that officials would think they were a man.

This also didn't stop some women, who somehow hadn't been removed from the register for the general election which would take place a month later, on the 17th of November 1868, from voting. Over two hundred women remained on registers throughout the country, and over ninety of them voted. All of these women's votes were later declared illegal and were not allowed to stand.

The following year, although women still couldn't vote in Parliamentary elections, the Municipal Franchise Act of 1869 resulted in women who met the property qualification being legally entitled to vote in municipal elections, but not in Parliamentary elections.

Following the 1867 controversy, electoral registers were more carefully scrutinised by officials for women's names, and when these were found they were removed. Despite increased scrutiny, women's names continued to slip through the net. This was particularly so for widows and single women who paid rates and who had names similar to men's names.

1874 – 1876

A general election was called in 1874 by William Gladstone, a Liberal. The Liberals lost to the Conservatives, headed by Benjamin Disraeli. This was the first time that the Conservatives had won since 1841, and the first general election since the 1872 Secret Ballot Act was introduced following allegations of voter bribery. Prior to this, people openly declared who they were voting for. This was entered into a polling book, which was open to public viewing. Following the Secret Ballot Act, voters placed a cross against the candidate of their choice and placed their ballot paper into a sealed box — the same as we do now.

During the 1874 general election, which was held throughout the UK between the 31st of January and the 17th of February, a woman voted at Bury and another at Salford. Neither of these women's names was found in the newspaper report, which merely stated that two women had voted — *Sheffield Evening Telegraph* August 1895.

It seemed that no one wanted to draw the public's attention to women voters. It is also possible that these women's votes were submitted through tendered papers and later declared illegal under the previous court ruling.

In 1867, Lilly Maxwell voted for Mr Jacob Bright, a Liberal, who won his seat at the Manchester by-election. Lilly Maxwell's vote was later discounted. But, in 1876, yet another woman voted for Mr Bright. Christian Donald, a householder, cast her vote successfully in the Manchester by-election held on the 19th of February. Jacob Bright won the seat.

The by-election was caused by the death of William Romaine Callender, Conservative MP.

1880—1883

The 1880 general election was held between the 31st of March and the 27th of April. The Liberals, headed by William Gladstone, won the election and secured one of their largest ever majorities replacing Benjamin Disraeli, a Conservative.

Newspaper reports indicate that many women's names were entered onto the list of electors in the 1880 general election, and many of these women voted. An article in the *Woman's Suffrage Journal*, reported that this happened with a certainty in Manchester, Oldham, Salford, South East Lancashire, East Redford and possibly in other constituencies in England. These women received ballot papers and deposited them in the ballot box. Who these women were is unclear.

A by-election was held in Manchester on the 4th of October 1883 and was brought about by the death of Mr Hugh Birley, Conservative MP. The defeat of Doctor Pankhurst, Independent Liberal, took up most of the newspaper headlines. Mr Houldsworth, Conservative, won the seat by a great majority.

At a meeting prior to the election, reported in the *Manchester Courier and Lancashire General Advertiser*, 4th of October, a presiding officer, Mr W. Batty, asked what should be done if a woman, whose name was on the register, presented herself to vote. Alderman, Sir Thomas Baker, said that no woman had the right to record their vote.

1885 – 1888

In 1885, the first general election was held following the introduction of the Representation of the People Act 1884 — The 'Third Reform Act'— which extended the franchise to more men.

The 1884 Act replaced the 1867 Reform Act — which judges had ruled didn't apply to women. Under the conditions of the 1867 Reform Act, the women's votes were declared illegal by the Court of Common Pleas and the loophole was plugged. But this ruling would not apply under the new 1884 Reform Act. Effectively, the loophole had been unplugged.

The general election was held between the 24th of November and the 18th of December. The Liberals, led by William Gladstone, won the election — but not with an overall majority. Gladstone was opposed to women's suffrage.

An article in the *Sheffield Evening Telegraph*, on the 24th August 1895, *'A Confusion of Christian Names'*, reports that a number of women voted in the election of 1885. Thomasine Westoe voted in Sacriston, Mid Durham, and Kesiah Jackson voted at Hull. And, in the Stretford Division of Lancashire, Mrs Jessie Walker voted. In Derbyshire, Jessie Russell did the same. There are no further details provided about these women, or who they voted for.

A by-election was held in Coventry on the 9th of July 1887. William Ballantine, a Liberal, won the seat. The election was caused by the elevation to the peerage of the Conservative MP, Henry Eaton (as Lord Cheylesmore), who had won the seat in the general election of the previous year.

At least one woman voted in the Coventry by-election. Jesse Johnson presented herself at one of the polling stations and claimed her right to vote. Her name was listed on the electoral register. The presiding officer initially rejected her claim, but after obtaining a legal opinion from the presiding barrister, he accepted it — *Exeter and Plymouth Gazette* 12th of July.

At this time, women's suffrage campaigners were drawn from the middle and upper classes. In July 1888, 1,400 match workers from Bow in East London, mostly women, went on strike against their working conditions at the Bryant & May factories.

40. Procession of Match Workers to Westminster, July 1888.

Despite working fourteen-hours a day, the women rarely received their weekly wage of a few shillings — as a result of the heavy financial fines imposed on them for petty offences such as dropping matches or talking. They also suffered ill-effects from exposure to the phosphorous they used to make the matches — yellowed skin, hair loss, vomiting and phossy jaw (a lethal necrotic form of bone cancer).

The formation of the Union of Women Match Makers, led by Mrs Annie Besant, marked the start of working–class women's involvement in the women's suffrage movement.

41. Mrs Annie Besant with the Matchgirls Strike Committee in 1888.

1892 General Election

In the run up to the 1892 general election, a Woman's Suffrage Bill which was due to be read for the second time in Parliament was postponed. The election was held between the 4th and the 26th of July. William Gladstone, a Liberal, returned for a fourth term as Prime Minister. He remained openly opposed to women's suffrage.

At least two women voted in the general election. Alma Pearce voted in the Mid-division of Gloucestershire, and, Jeannet Edwards voted in Montgomeryshire. No further information is provided in the article in the *Sheffield Evening Telegraph*, 24th August 1895.

1900 General Election

The general election of 1900 was held between the 26th of September and the 24th of October. The Conservative and Liberal Unionists, led by Lord Salisbury, won the election by a large majority. A woman, Mrs Jessie Gill, voted in the Fareham Division of Hampshire. The woman's husband, Alfred, was on active service in Africa. According to a report in the *Evening Star,* 9th October, at first the presiding officer refused to allow her to cast her vote. Mrs Gill persisted and was eventually given a ballot paper.

Two days later, in South East Essex, Miss Julia Leaver turned up to cast her vote. Her name was on the electoral register and she had been sent a polling card. When she tried to vote for Mr Whitehead, the Liberal candidate, the presiding officer refused—*London Daily News,* Thursday 11 October.

Men were not immune from clerical errors on the electoral register. A man whose Christian name was Louis was entered onto the register as Louisa, he was not allowed to cast his vote—*Liverpool Mercury*, September 1900.

1906 General Election

The 1906 general election was held between the 12th January and the 8th of February. The Liberal Party, led by Henry Campbell-Bannerman, won the election with a large majority, replacing the coalition Government — between the Conservative and Liberal

Unionist parties — which had governed the country for ten years, since the general election of 1895.

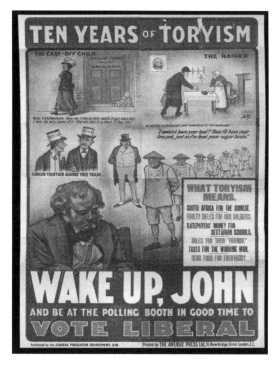

42. Ten years of Toryism poster. Produced by the Liberal Party for the 1906 election. The poster shows the Tory record during their government over the last ten years.

More women were reported as having voted in this election than in any previous one. The names of at least nine women appeared on electoral registers throughout England.

A huge error also occurred in the Eccles division of South-East Lancashire. About 1,500 women's names were accidentally added to the Parliamentary register, instead of the local register. The mistake, which was reported in the *Sheffield Evening Telegraph* on the 10th of January, was quickly rectified.

Alwyn Bussey was the first woman to vote in the general election of that year, earning her the title in the newspapers as 'England's only woman voter.' Her name appeared on the electoral register for East Marylebone in London.

On the 15th of January, Alwyn Bussey turned up to cast her vote at the Little Titchfield Street Polling Station. It would seem that the name Alwyn caused the source of the confusion and she was placed on the register in the belief that she was a man. She was a widow who rented a studio in Wells Street where she taught singing.

She became one of the most talked about women in London, as the only woman to have voted in a Parliamentary election. Stories circulated as far as America as to how she attended. Some newspaper reports there said that she went disguised as a man.

Alwyn Bussey was interviewed by a reporter from the *Daily Mirror*. As amusing as the incident was to her, she confessed to the reporter, as she sat at her piano in her music studio at 66 Wells Street in Oxford Circus, that she was quite upset by the publicity. *'I'm told I'm the only woman who ever voted for a Parliamentary candidate. From Christmas, I began to get great quantities of campaign literature. Most of it went into the fire. When I received papers addressed 'A. Bussey, Esq.,' I determined to vote.'*

On the day of the election, a two-horse carriage arrived at Alwyn Bussey's door to transport her to the polling station. She said that when she arrived there, that was when the trouble started. Even the policeman laughed at her and told her that women couldn't vote. The presiding officer refused to give her a ballot paper and asked her to come back in the afternoon, once he had time to look into the books. However, one of the other presiding officers reminded him that they could not refuse to give a polling paper to anyone whose name was on the electoral register and she was duly given one—becoming the first woman to vote in a Parliamentary election in Marylebone.

Miss Bussey had moved to London from Germany eight years before. Her story was also published in the *Taunton Courier and Western Advertiser* on the 17th of January and in the *Leeds Mercury* on the 18th. A photograph of Alwyn Bussey is included in an article in the *Sketch*, 24th of January. The picture shows a glamorous woman with light-brown hair swept up onto the top of her head and pinned in place with what looks like a feather clasp. She is wearing a jewelled necklace with matching earrings and her dress is low cut and edged with, what looks to be, silk flowers.

However, it was a case of while one woman was allowed to vote, another woman was not.

On the 18th of January, the *Leeds Mercury* reported that a seventy-four-year-old seamstress, Mrs Eliza Chamberlain of Fox Court, Gray's Inn Road, Holborn, London, had discovered that her name was on the electoral register. Eliza Chamberlain was aware that a woman teacher, Mrs Alwyn Bussey had voted in East Marleybone. So, after finishing work for the day, she trudged through the rain to the Laystall Street polling station and demanded her voting ticket. The presiding officer refused on the grounds that no woman was allowed to vote.

Mrs Chamberlain argued that if Miss Bussey had a vote in Marleybone, why should she not have one in Holborn? *'Although I am an old woman, I mean to assert my rights.'* The presiding officer stuck to his decision. And, much disappointed, Eliza Chamberlain left without voting.

In 1911, Frances Connelly's name was placed on the register through a clerical error when her name was misspelt as Francis. But, she wasn't the first woman with the name Frances who was placed on the register through a clerical error.

A woman voted in Berwick-upon Tweed, an English town close to the border with Scotland. Mrs Frances Kinross, from Castlegate, was the mother of the schoolmaster at Paxton. It is believed her name had been placed on the register through the misspelling of her Christian name as Francis. According to a brief report in the *Berwickshire News & General Advertiser*, 30th January, after receiving her voting paper Mrs Kinross went to the polling station in Berwick Town Hall and recorded her vote for Sir Edward Grey, Liberal. Sir Grey won the seat.

And, on the 18th of January, 1906, Frances Wright (misspelt as Francis) turned up at the polling station in the Eastern Division of Nottingham and was allowed to register her vote.

The *Portsmouth Evening News* Friday the 19th January 1906, reported that a woman had voted in Poole and another in Baildon, but there is no mention of their names in the brief report about this.

Yet another woman in 1906 claimed the distinction of having voted in a Parliamentary election. A widow, Maud James of

Beeston, voted in the Rushcliffe division of Nottinghamshire. After her husband died Maud James took over occupancy of the house. When the electoral register was drawn up her name was reversed, and it appeared on the list as James Maud. On the day of the election, a canvasser informed her about the error. She immediately expressed her determination to vote, and arrived at the polling station to loud cheers – *Sheffield Evening Telegraph*, 25th January.

There was also a brief account in the *Portsmouth Evening News* on the 22nd of January, about three other women who voted. Mrs Jessie Vine, a shopkeeper from Kent, and Mrs Millbank of Bush Hill Park, London, recorded their votes. And a woman's name was discovered on the register for the poll at the Wimbledon division of Surrey, which was yet to take place.

1908 Wolverhampton East by-election

The Wolverhampton East by-election was necessitated by the elevation to the peerage of Henry Hartley Fowler, Liberal MP. The election was held on the 5th of May. The Liberals held the seat. George Rennie Thorne won by a narrow majority of eight votes.

The Women's Freedom League (WFL) had placed some of their members at each of the electoral stations within the constituency. Throughout the day the women canvassed on behalf of Leopold Amery, the Unionist candidate, and urged electors to vote against the Liberal Government.

Due to a clerical error, a working-class woman was entered on the electoral register for Wolverhampton East, as Louis Dawson instead of Lois Dawson. Lois Dawson voted. The discovery that a woman's name was on the Parliamentary register was relayed to Mrs Manson, of the National Society for Women's Suffrage. The story of this 'Suffragist triumph' was picked up by many newspapers at the time, including the *Daily Telegraph & Courier (London)* and the *Dundee Evening Telegraph* in Scotland.

According to newspaper reports, when Lois Dawson emerged triumphant from the booth the suffragettes who were outside, seized her in a paroxysm of joy, hugged her, and offered congratulations. The Unionist candidate, Mr Leopold Amery, who was in the district at the time, shook Lois Dawson by the hand.

Lois Dawson's vote was also mentioned in the *Northampton Daily Record* on the 5th of May, as a 'Suffragist triumph.' And in *The Globe* on the same day, a member of the Women's Freedom League commented, '*If one woman can vote, why not all?*'

The *Sheffield Evening Telegraph*, Tuesday 5th of May, headlined the announcement of Lois Dawson's vote with—*Woman's Triumph. Allowed To Record a Vote*, and reported—

'The Women's Freedom League announced that a lady recorded her vote at the Parliamentary election in East Wolverhampton this morning. The voter's name is Lois Dawson. It appears that she was down in the register as Louis. This interesting discovery was made by Mrs Mcason, the lady clerk in charge of the committee rooms of the Women's Freedom League in the constituency. The elector recorded her vote amid general excitement. She was conveyed in triumph to the poll by the Suffragettes.'

The event was reported as a 'Suffragist Triumph'. *'The East Wolverhampton election will be remembered if only from the fact that a woman had the vote. The incident occurred in the Redcross Street district. The name Louis Dawson, ... was upon the register. A woman claimed it and voted.'*

Lois Dawson's name had been on the electoral register for twelve years, but she hadn't been aware that she could vote. After she voted, the Women's Freedom League wired a Telegram to the Prime Minister, Mr Asquith, informing him, 'Polled woman voter. Register number 1218. Red Cross Street School, Wolverhampton Election. Election here being fought on the Franchise Bill.'

The by-election proved a near disaster for the Liberals. There was talk at the time of demanding a scrutiny of the poll due to the narrow win, but this does not appear to have taken place. If it had, according to newspaper reports, there seemed little doubt that Lois Dawson's vote would have been discarded.

Born in Longton, North Staffordshire, Lois Dawson lived at the time of her vote at 15 Red-Hill Street, Staffordshire. The 1911 census shows her as sixty-seven-years-old (born 1844) and a widow who had been married for thirty-three years. She was living with her daughter also Lois (a twenty-four-year-old colour worker with a paint manufacturer) and two boarders —Alfred Webb (70) and Howard Randell (32).

Although it was obvious a mistake had been made, the poll clerks had no option but to accept Lois Dawson's vote. The Women's

Freedom League had raised a pertinent question, if one woman can vote why not all?

1909 Croydon by-election

The by-election was held due to the death of the Liberal Unionist MP for Croydon, H.O. Arnold-Forster. The election took place on the 29th of March. The seat was won by the Conservative candidate, Robert Hermon-Hodge.

The London Daily News, March the 29th issue, reported that two women's names had been found on the electoral register for the by-election which would take place that day. Joy Channon refused to vote or be interviewed by the press. The second woman, who was from Thornton Heath, refused to have her name and address released, but said she would vote Liberal.

Two women from the Women's Freedom League, Mrs Holmes and Miss Muriel Matters, approached the Mayor and asked if it was legal in the constituency to nominate a candidate and if they could hold over nominations until they could do so. According to a report in the *Leeds Mercury*, 25th March, the women were told no by the Mayor, who explained that the presiding officer had no power to hold back the election.

1910 General Elections

Two general elections were held in 1910. The first election was held in January and the second in December.

David Lloyd George's People's Budget (to raise funds through taxes to pay for social reforms) had passed through the House of Commons on the 3rd of November 1909. But, on the 30th, the House of Lords rejected the budget, forcing a general election.

January 1910 General Election

The first general election of 1910, held between the 5th of January and the 10th of February, resulted in a reduced Liberal majority.

A woman voted at the Beckenham District of London in the Sevenoaks Division. According to the *Buckingham Advertiser and Free Press*, 22nd January, Mrs Montie Arnold, the widow of a music-hall artist, was given a ballot paper and her .vote was counted along with the others.

Once again, while one woman was allowed to vote another was not.

Mrs Wilson Edwards of 188, Earlham Road, Norwich, whose name appeared in the voters register for the Norwich constituency, presented herself at the polling station on the 17th of January, but she wasn't allowed to vote—reported in the *Shepton Mallet Journal* 21st January.

According to a report in the *Gloucester Citizen*, January 18th, Mrs Edwards had been conveyed to the polling station in a motor-car provided by the Conservatives. The returning officer refused to give Mrs Edwards a polling ticket, stating that, 'definite instructions had been given to every presiding officer in Norwich and Norfolk that women were not to be admitted'. After much fuss, and very disappointed, Mrs Wilson Edwards left without voting.

Although no name is given, an article in the *Dundee Evening Telegraph*, January 25th, reported that a woman at Bootle recorded a vote for the Conservative candidate, and a Liberal objection was lodged.

December 1910 General Election

In March, King Edward VII, a heavy smoker, became extremely ill with bronchitis. By April, the King's health had declined further. He died on the 6th of May and was succeeded by his son, George V.

A Bill to stop the House of Lords vetoing legislation was introduced in the Commons on the 4th of April, starting a clash between the Lords and the Commons.

David Lloyd George's (1909) 'People's Budget' was passed by the House of Commons for the second time on the 27th of April, and by the House of Lords on the 29th of April.

On the 18th of November, 'Black Friday', hundreds of suffragettes clashed with police outside Parliament over the failure of the Bill to Extend the Parliamentary Franchise to women who owned or rented property. Four men and one hundred and fifteen women were arrested. All charges were dropped.

The second general election of 1910 was held between the 3rd and 19th of December, resulting in a Liberal majority. The election was called in order to pass a mandate for the Parliament Act 1911—to prevent the House of Lords from blocking legislation passed by the

House of Commons. This was the last election in which voting took place over several days and the last general election in which women couldn't vote.

1911 South Somerset by-election

Frances Connelly recorded her vote in the South Somerset by-election in November, earning her the title of the first woman voter in Yeovil. Newspapers report that her vote was counted along with the others, and not through a tendered ballot paper.

1912 Bow and Bromley by-election

In 1911, protests by workers seeking to secure a minimum wage escalated to a scale never seen before in the UK. Around nine hundred strikes took place; including the dock and rail strikes. In 1912, unrest continued to spread throughout the workforce. Thousands of workers joined in the industrial action, including the jute workers in Dundee, Scotland, taxicab drivers in London and the cotton weavers in Lancashire. Troops were deployed against the striking workers. Then, at the end of February 1912, a million miners voted to take part in a national strike. Fearful of a worker's revolt, a revolution, the Government hurried a minimum wage Bill through Parliament.

The Bow and Bromley (a constituency in London) by-election was held on the 26th of November. The by-election was caused by the resignation of George Lansbury, Labour MP. George Lansbury was a strong supporter of women's suffrage and the WSPU. He strongly disagreed with the policy of force-feeding women who went on hunger strike in prison.

Enraged by the Government's refusal to intervene to halt the force-feeding of women, Lansbury had reacted with an angry outburst in the House of Commons, directed at the Prime Minister, Asquith.

Lansbury resigned his seat for Bow and Bromley to highlight the issue of women's suffrage. Although he was supported by the WSPU (suffragettes), the NUWSS leaders (suffragists), refused to take part in Lansbury's campaign.

It rained heavily on the day of the election. Carriages had been donated by WSPU members in the area to transport voters to the polling station. But, a group of suffragettes refused to hand over the WSPU carriages to Lansbury's supporters, on the grounds that the Pankhursts would never support a campaign run by men. By the time things were sorted out, Lansbury had lost critical time and voters. He also lost the seat.

Lansbury had stood as an Independent Labour candidate (supporting votes for women). The Labour Party had not endorsed him as their candidate or stand another candidate. The Liberals did not stand a candidate either. Reginald Blair, Conservative, won the by-election by a majority vote. Blair was supported by the National League for Opposing Women Suffrage. His campaign included the slogan, 'Women do not want votes.'

One woman, Unity Dorking, voted in the by-election. A report in the *Pall Mall Gazette* on the 27th of November noted that she voted against the candidate who stood for votes for women —Lansbury. Unusually for the time, a picture of Unity Dorking was included in the report.

General Election 1918

Soon after the end of the First World War, the first General Election since 1910 was called. The election was held on Saturday the 14th of December, 1918.

It was the first general election to take place on a single day, although the vote count was delayed until the 28th of December to allow the votes cast by soldiers serving overseas to be included.

The election resulted in a landslide victory for the coalition government of David Lloyd George, who had replaced Henry Herbert Asquith as Prime Minister in December 1916.

It was also the first general election to be held after the enactment of the Representation of the People Act 1918. It was, therefore, the first time in which all propertied or university educated women over the age of thirty and all men over the age of twenty-one could vote in a Parliamentary election in the UK.

There was a 57% turnout. Women accounted for about 43% of the electorate (8.5 million women).

There was no longer a need now for women to be recorded in the newspapers as having been placed on the electoral register in error. But, in the main, women who had slipped through the net and voted before this were working-class women.

In 1928, the Conservative Government passed the Representation of the People (Equal Franchise) Act giving the vote to all men and women over the age of twenty-one. This was lowered in 1970, to eighteen.

Having the same voting rights as men was an entitlement that was fought for by women and not, as is often implied, a privilege extended to them. When some women of means were finally free to vote in 1918, the names of many working-class suffrage activists and supporters who had helped them win the fight were often forgotten. Hopefully, more of their names will appear in the 1928 celebrations to mark the centenary of all women over the age of twenty-one gaining the right to vote in Parliamentary elections in the UK.

In the ten years, between 1918 until the 1928 People's Act was passed, enfranchising all women over the age of twenty-one, it is likely that many more disenfranchised women continued to have their names added to the electoral register through clerical errors. But, their names, amidst the names of eligible women voters, would have been harder, if not impossible to detect.

WOMEN WHO VOTED BEFORE 1918

Women's suffrage was led by many remarkable women who were, by-and-large, wealthy and well-connected. Frances Connelly, a working-class woman from Yeovil, was neither wealthy nor well-connected. Despite this, by voting in a Parliamentary election before an Act had been passed enabling her to do so, Frances Connelly truly carried out the call for 'deeds and not words'.

Rather than pass up an opportunity provided to her by chance, Frances Connelly, in making the conscious decision to exercise a right that had been denied to her and all women in the UK at the time, did something extraordinary for women's suffrage.

In 1911, Frances Connelly was the first woman in Yeovil to vote in a Parliamentary election.

Lilly Maxwell voted in 1867, but her vote was later declared illegal by the courts. Around ninety women followed Lilly Maxwell's example and got their names onto the register for the general election in 1868. All were declared void and illegal by the courts.

Since then, many women were accidentally sent a polling card. Some of these women did not want to vote. Some, like the seventy-four-year-old seamstress, Eliza Chamberlain, turned up to vote but were refused. Some women were brought to the polling station by members of the women's suffrage movement and cast their vote. Others, like Frances Connelly, argued for their right to vote and this was granted.

Despite attempts to close the loophole, women continued to slip through the net and voted in the general election of 1906 and the two general elections held in 1910 (January and December). Women also voted in some by-elections.

Regardless of who was first past the post, to earn the title of the first woman to vote in the UK, all of these women had the courage to cast their vote in a Parliamentary election before the law entitled them to do so. As such, Frances Connelly and the other women who voted deserve recognition for the contribution they made to women's suffrage in the UK. Had they been women of means or active members of the suffrage movement it is likely that their votes would have received more attention and newspaper coverage at the time.

FRANCES CONNELY

Illness and Death

On the 23rd of March 1917, six years after casting her vote in the South Somerset by-election, Frances Connelly died. She was forty-nine-years-old.

Frances didn't live to see the first women voting in the 1918 general election. Nor did she live to hear about the Act that was passed by Parliament enabling some women to do so. On the 28th March, 1917, five days after Frances died, the House of Commons voted with an overwhelming majority that women over the age of thirty who were householders, the wives of householders, occupiers of property with an annual rent of £5 or educated at a British university could legally vote in UK Parliamentary elections. And, in December 1918, this select group of women had their first opportunity to vote in a UK General Election.

With her son, Walter James Connelly, beside her, Frances died at home, at 1 Salisbury Terrace, Reckleford, Yeovil. The cause of death is recorded as Pulmonary Phthisis — the old term for Pulmonary Tuberculosis (TB). At this time, TB was commonly called consumption — because of the weight loss associated with the illness.

Although Frances was referred to as a widow in a newspaper report in 1911, on her death certificate it stated, 'Wife of Edward Connelly, Hotel Manager.'

There was no mention of Frances's youngest son, Edward Arthur Connelly. He was born in Islington, London in 1898, making him around 19-20 years of age at the time of Frances's death. Edward was conscripted in to the army in August 1916, aged eighteen, as a Private, and most likely would have been serving abroad. He was discharged from the army in May 1919.

Frances's son, William, married Maud Alice Pennell. In the 1939 register, they are listed as living at 1 Salisbury Terrace, Reckleford (Frances's previous home address). William was working as an aircraft operative heavy worker on night shift.

In 1926, Frances's son, Walter, married Emily Young (born 1892). In the 1939 register, the family are listed as living in Lower Vagg, Yeovil. Walter was working as a leather wheeler in the gloving industry (operating a wheel used on wet skins to produce a suede finish).

Frances Connelly

Frances's mother outlived her, dying the following year in 1918.

Although Frances didn't live to see the start of women's enfranchisement, she did have the satisfaction of casting her own vote in a Parliamentary election and having it counted.

Rather than remaining a forgotten figure in the centenary celebrations of some women gaining the vote in the UK, Frances Connelly should be remembered amongst those who had the courage to fight to exercise her right to do so.

ONE HUNDRED YEARS LATER

The Re-reporting of Yeovil's first Woman Voter by Laura Linham

Over a hundred years after the event was originally reported, Laura Linham, a senior reporter with Somerset Live, uncovered and revealed Frances Connelly's incredible story online in January 2017, and followed this up in her article on the 22nd of May 2017; *'Frances Connelly: The Yeovil woman who made history voting seven years before it was legal.'*

Without Laura's report, it is possible that these amazing events would have remained archived. Laura explains what led her to write the article.

Frances' story had remained hidden on a quiet corner of the internet—in Bob Osborn's wonderful resource, The A-to-Z of Yeovil's History - http://www.yeovilhistory.info/index.htm/

I had just been through a restructure after the paper I worked for was bought out. The office I'd worked in had been moved to Yeovil, so I took advantage of Mr Osborn's research to find out more about the town I would be working in.

It is to my regret that for the longest time — like much of the rest of the world — I ignored Frances Connelly's story — which was filed neatly away in a list of notable people from Yeovil's past, from rope and twine makers to traders and solicitors and shop owners. A list of the great and the good from the town — but perhaps no-one you'd think of as exceptional.

And so, I kept skipping over Frances Connelly's entry, assuming that she was a rich land-owner who, while being notable as the first woman in Yeovil to vote, hadn't really done anything out of the ordinary.

So, when I finally did get around to reading Frances Connelly's story — brief as the entry was — I was instantly intrigued and headed straight for the newspaper archives to dig out the story for myself. The more I read, the more I couldn't believe that Frances Connelly's story wasn't better known.

I chatted this through with my editor — who thought I might be onto something — and then spent an instructive few hours in the archives hunting down Frances's story.

Oddly, even back then, there wasn't that much on Frances Connelly. The significance of this woman's quiet protest — walking into the polling station and putting her 'X' on the paper warranted a rare photograph in the Western Gazette. Very few photos were included at that time, especially in newspapers which were wall to wall text, a few column inches, but little more. Frances Connelly's story did not spread to the bigger newspapers of the time — presumably in case her story encouraged those 'pesky' suffragettes — and she faded away into obscurity.

The article was published online, and Frances Connelly was once again in the pages of the Western Gazette. While the story didn't really set the world on fire, a news agency I worked with spotted the story, picked it up and sent it on to the nationals. At the end of January 2017, the Independent, Telegraph, Daily Mail, and before long, a few other news sites, had picked it up and featured it on their websites.

While more people had now read Frances Connelly's story, it still didn't seem enough to me, somehow. At this time, I'd become increasingly frustrated at the state of British politics and even more frustrated by low voter turnouts at the polls — a little under 69 per cent of people eligible to vote at the 2017 election actually did so, and social media posts of people saying they weren't going to vote because 'their vote didn't matter' drove me crazy.

Women had fought so long and so hard for the right to have their say in who they wanted to run the country and in a relatively short space of time people seemed to have become blasé.

For me, Frances Connelly's story was so much more interesting because of who she was, or rather who she wasn't. Frances wasn't a trailblazing politician or a prominent suffragist. She hadn't been educated at an elite school and wasn't a member of the upper classes.

It had been a clerical error which had given Frances, a working-class woman from Yeovil, an opportunity and she grabbed that opportunity. The moment she put that X on her paper, Frances Connelly could have been guaranteed a place in the history books—but having been denied the right to vote, she was also denied her place in history — thanks to the men who were most likely writing it at the time.

So when I was contacted to ask if I would co-author this book featuring Frances Connelly on behalf of the One Million Project (OMP) and that more than 100 years later, Frances might finally get the recognition she deserved for flying in the face of authority, I couldn't have been happier to get involved.

KEEPING FRANCES CONNELLY'S NAME ALIVE
Sally A Barr—Artist

Sally A. Barr is a UK based artist and illustrator. She works mainly in acrylic paint but explores mediums such as watercolour and charcoal among others.

As a woman who was raised surrounded by an old-fashioned mindset, regarding a woman's options, Sally felt incredibly justified in her rebellious reactions, to be present at a march marking 100 years of the woman's vote. She attended the march in London on the 10th of June 2018, carrying a banner made from her portrait of Frances Connelly, with her eldest daughter and thousands of empowered women and girls.

43. The banner carried by Sally A Barr at the 100 year anniversary celebration march for women getting the vote in London on the 10th of June 2018.

The atmosphere during the march was electric, but Sally's favourite moment was when she was approached by a group of girls, around twelve-years-old, asking to buy a postcard souvenir of her painting of Frances Connelly. She explained to them who Frances Connelly was and told them how Frances came to be the first woman to vote in Yeovil and have her vote counted and stand, and how she came to be amongst the first women to do so in the UK.

The girls were captivated. Their reaction and genuine interest is exactly why Sally believes we need to keep Frances Connelly's name alive. She said, '*Frances could quite easily have opted out of voting, amidst severe opposition, but she didn't. I can only imagine how liberating this must have been.*'

44. Painting of Frances Connelly by Sally A. Barr, 2017.

Sally explains the above painting of Frances Connelly which is also featured on the front cover of this book:

'The painting is a combination of fluid and strong, using suffragette colours for the background. It seemed fitting to portray Frances as a strong silhouette almost like the head of a stamp. I used acrylic paint and a blowtorch to achieve the effects I wanted.'

45. Picture of Artist- Sally A Barr, 2018

Sally looks forward to a day when women can just be, not questioned, compared or criticised for their choices. She feels incredibly privileged to be the contributing artist in this book and says, 'It addresses a subject very close to my heart as with many women who have faced trials and tribulations as a matter of course, for being an underestimated woman.

Yeovil & Sherborne Soroptimists

Soroptimist International is the world's largest service organisation for women, working through projects to educate, enable and empower women and girls.

The organisation has an active branch in Yeovil and Sherborne which supports the women in the towns and villages in the surrounding areas. It has a lively and diverse group of women members.

In December 2015, as part of the organisation's Fearless campaign, to draw attention to extraordinary and often overlooked women, they were set a challenge to put a t-shirt and sash on the statue of a woman who deserved to be celebrated.

However, it wasn't long before the group discovered an issue with this particular challenge – there were no statues of any women in Somerset or Dorset. In fact, the only statue they could find marking the achievements of a woman was a statue of Queen Victoria in Bristol – far off their patch.

In fact, the campaign did have the unexpected result of highlighting some depressing figures —according to The Public Monuments and Sculpture Association, of the 828 statues of people across the UK they have recorded 174 of them were female—around one in five.

Taking Headless Woman (Nymph), Woman Taking off Dress or any of four caryatids out of the equation, even among the eighty female figures with names fifteen are allegorical, mythical or otherwise fictional.

And thirty-eight of those statues are royal, with Queen Victoria being the woman most commonly memorialised.

Faced with these figures, the Soroptimists in Yeovil posed outside of what was once the Town Hall where Frances cast her vote and announced a campaign to bring a statue of Frances to the town.

Although the campaign has borne little fruit at the time of writing, the group have high hopes that the town will one day find some way to honour Frances Connelly.

1918 AND BEYOND

In 1918, when the 'Representation of the People Act' was passed, the age for male voters was lowered to twenty-one (nineteen for servicemen), while only some women over the age of thirty were included. With more adult women than men in the population at this time (the difference had steadily grown between 1901 and 1918), if all adult women had been included in the Act then more women than men would have been eligible to vote in Parliamentary elections. As it was, in the next General election in 1918, 57% of the electorate voted. Over 40% of the names on the electoral register were women. Never again could it be said that women were not interested in politics.

Some suffrage campaigners hailed the 1918 Act as a victory and turned their attention to new roles for women, including becoming Members of Parliament and entering professions previously denied to them. The fight for universal suffrage seemed to have been all but forgotten by them.

Although there is less information readily available, many women's suffrage groups did continue to campaign beyond the introduction of the 1918 Act. Their focus, however, turned to gaining equal enfranchisement, and new groups formed.

For working-class women, who remained disenfranchised, the period following 1918 was marked by high unemployment and recession throughout the country. The Unemployment Insurance Act, which was passed in 1920, provided them with lower benefits than men, and women who worked in domestic service were paid nothing at all.

Splits had occurred within the suffrage movement, and some groups had already disbanded. The onset of war had splintered the suffrage movement into those who were for and those who were against it, and this brought to a head the rumbling disagreements about who suffrage should be fought for—women on the same basis as men, or all adults. These splits were felt most within the suffragette movement.

The Women's Social and Political Union (WSPU) turned towards helping with the war effort and took little part in the continued suffrage movement. Although the majority of WSPU members supported the war, a small number did not. The WSPU was finally dissolved in 1917, changing its name to the Women's Party—a minor political party.

Although many of the key suffrage leaders had turned away from the fight for universal suffrage, many suffrage groups continued to fight for full suffrage for women and for equal rights in the workplace, mainly through involvement in trade unions.

After splitting from the WSPU in 1914, the East London Federation of Suffragettes (ELFS) formed, led by Sylvia Pankhurst. In 1916 the ELFS changed its name to the Worker's Suffrage

Federation (WSF) and began fighting for enfranchisement for all adult men and women and formed branches throughout England, Scotland and Wales. After the 1918 Act was passed, the WSF changed its name again—becoming the Workers' Socialist Federation which continued campaigning for women to have the same right to vote as men and worked on other equality issues that affected working-class women. The WSF disbanded in 1924.

In 1919, the National Union of Women's Suffrage Societies (NUWSS), a suffragist organisation, renamed itself as the National Union of Societies for Equal Citizenship (NUSEC) and continued to campaign for equal voting rights for women.

Throughout the years leading up to 1918, many working-class women had been militant in their fight for women's suffrage. Imprisonment wasn't an easy option for them. While their affiliated suffrage groups often paid bail to have them released from prison, no bail was allowed for more serious offences.

Many of the contributions from these and numerous other women have now largely been forgotten. A small fraction of their many stories have been mentioned here within the context of Frances Connelly's story. The names of many other working-class women remain confined to the archives. Unless their names appeared in reports or newspaper accounts at the time, there is often frustratingly little recorded about them to tell.

As the centenary of some women gaining the right to vote in 1918 is celebrated, the sacrifices made by many ordinary women, who also fought for equality for all women, should be acknowledged alongside those who were better off than them.

Many who campaigned for women's suffrage also wanted to change long-held views about women's inequality with men. In trying to achieve this, many women (and some men) endured great personal sacrifice. Many lost their jobs, homes, families, and some even lost their lives.

Finally, on the 7th of May 1928, the Representation of the People Act was passed lowering the voting age for women from thirty to twenty-one and removing the property qualification. From the 2nd of July, women had equal status with men to vote in Parliamentary elections. The Act was passed by the Conservative party, with minimal opposition.

All women over the age of twenty-one were able to vote in the 1929 general election which was held on Thursday the 30th of May. There was a 76% turnout, and 52% of the names on the electoral register were women.

Seventeen years before the 1928 Act, Frances Connelly was provided with the opportunity to vote in a Parliamentary election while the laws prevented her from doing so. She grabbed this chance with both hands. And, having made her mark, Frances proudly left the polling station.

In voting that day, Frances Connelly, along with the many other women who voted before 1918, helped keep the question to the forefront of people's mind; if one woman can vote, why not all?

PICTURE CREDITS

Photograph of Frances Connelly by Witcomb & Son Yeovil circa 1911. Featured in the Western Gazette on the 24th of November 1911.

1, 2, 3, 4, 9, 14, 18, 19, 20, A-to-Z of Yeovil's History - Bob Osborn. http://www.yeovilhistory.info/index.htm.

5. By Sam Hood - From the collections of the State ibrary of NSW http://www.acmssearch.sl.nsw.gov.au/search/itemDetailPaged.cgi?it emID=15423 (item) Public Domain, https://commons.wikimedia.org/w/index.php?curid=36447824

6. Public Domain, https://commons.wikimedia.org/w/index.php?curid=39046 Source: http://www.bfi.org.uk/collections/mk/gallery/pages/r01_01.html

7. By Peter Higgimbothom - http://www.cqout.com/item.asp?id=4872846, Public Domain, https://commons.wikimedia.org/wiki/File:Women_mealtime_st_pan cras_workhouse.jpg#/media/File:Women_mealtime_st_pancras_wor khouse.jpg/

8. By Liberal Publication Department [Public domain], via Wikimedia Commons - https://commons.wikimedia.org/w/index.php?curid=7112054/

10. British Government - Photograph Q 42036 from the collections of the Imperial War Museums. Public Domain, https://commons.wikimedia.org/w/index.php?curid=4033625/

11. Painting. Selling a Wife. By Thomas Rowlandson [Public domain], By Thomas Rowlandson - Web Gallery of Art: Image Info about artwork, Public Domain, https://commons.wikimedia.org/w/index.php?curid=15500619/

12. By Unknown - The Suffragette by Sylvia Pankhurst. New York: Source Book Press, 1970. First published by Sturgis & Walton Company, 1911. Facing p. 174., Public Domain, https://commons.wikimedia.org/wiki/File:WSPU_in_Kingsway.jpg#/media/File:WSPU_in_Kingsway.jpg/

13. By W. F. Winter - Schlesinger Library, RIAS, Harvard University - https://www.flickr.com/photos/schlesinger_library/16616194363/, No restrictions, https://commons.wikimedia.org/wiki/File:Votes_for_Workers,_ca._1907-1918._(16616194363).jpg#/media/

15. The "Terrible Twins" David Lloyd George and Winston Churchill in 1907 during the peak of their "radical phase" as social reformers. Unknown. Public domain. https://commons.wikimedia.org/wiki/File:ChurchillGeorge0001.jpg#/media/File:ChurchillGeorge0001.jpg.

16. Suffragettes gather at Manchester Census Lodge to boycott the 1911 census. By Johnny Cyprus - Own work, CC BY-SA 3.0, https://commons.wikimedia.org/w/index.php?curid=7253766/

17. Author Beatrice Cundy. Published by Williams and Norgate, London 1928- https://commons.wikimedia.org/wiki/File:Evelina_Haverfield.jpg#/media/File:Evelina_Haverfield.jpg/

21. By Uncredited. - UK parliament website - http://www.parliament.uk/about/living-heritage/transformingsociety/electionsvoting/womenvote/parliamentary-collections/collections-the-vote-and-after/representation-of-the-people-act-1918/, OGL 3, https://commons.wikimedia.org/wiki/File:Representation_of_the_People_Act_1918.jpg#/media/File:Representation_of_the_People_Act_1918.jpg/

22. 23. Daily Mirror Photographer.
https://commons.wikimedia.org/wiki/File:1907_arrest_of_Dora_The
wlis.jpg#/media/File:1907_arrest_of_Dora_Thewlis.jpg/

24. Home Office surveillance photo circa 1914. From a copy in the
National Portrait Gallery, London.
https://commons.wikimedia.org/wiki/File:Lilian_Lenton_1914.jpg#/
media/File:Lilian_Lenton_1914.jpg/

25. By Women's Social and Political Union...NOR. - Museum of
London, Public domain,
https://commons.wikimedia.org/wiki/File:Cat_and_Mouse_Act_Post
er_-_1914.jpg#/media/File:Cat_and_Mouse_Act_Poster_-_1914.jpg/

26. By Alfred Pearce (1855–1933) *nom de plume* "A Patriot". Public
Domain. http://www.historyextra.com/article/social-history/10-facts-
about-suffragettes.
https://commons.wikimedia.org/w/index.php?curid=70437901/

27. By Johnny Cyprus - Own work, Public domain, Mabel Capper
outside Bow Street Court.
https://commons.wikimedia.org/w/index.php?curid=7252346/

28. By Mabel Capper - Mabel Cappers WSPU prisoner's scrapbook,
Public Domain,
https://commons.wikimedia.org/w/index.php?curid=49548292/

29. By Men's Political Union for Women's Enfranchisement,
photographer unknown. The Women's Library@LSE. Public
domain, via Wikimedia Commons
https://commons.wikimedia.org/wiki/File:Hugh_Franklin_suffragist.
png

30. Printed inscription on reverse 'Copyright Central News, 5 New
Bridge St, London EC'. By LSE Library -
https://www.flickr.com/photos/lselibrary/22708291240/ No
restrictions,
https://commons.wikimedia.org/w/index.php?curid=52003578

31. By Colonel Linley Blathwayt - Bath in Time via book "What Can History Do" by Feminist Archive South, Public domain, https://commons.wikimedia.org/w/index.php?curid=67342947/

32. The family of Violet Ann Bland extended permission for this portrait to be uploaded – https://commons.wikimedia.org/wiki/File:Violet_Ann_Bland.jpg#/media/File:Violet_Ann_Bland.jpg/

33. By WSPU Flyer held by Elizabeth Crawford Public domain. https://womanandhersphere.com/2013/05/20/campaigning-for-the-vote-kate-frye-and-black-friday-november-1910/ https://commons.wikimedia.org/w/index.php?curid=67767063/

34. LSE Library - No restrictions. wspu_making banners. https://commons.wikimedia.org/wiki/File:WSPU_making_banners_(24206086987).jpg#/media/File:WSPU_making_banners_(24206086987).jpg/

35. The Daily Mirror, 19th November 1910, page 11. Public domain, https://commons.wikimedia.org/w/index.php?curid=67767812/

36. Victor Consolé. From File:Black Friday, London, 18 November 1910, suffragette attacked.jpg, added in this edit.) - Archives of The Daily Mirror, Public domain, https://commons.wikimedia.org/wiki/File:Black_Friday,_attacked_suffragette_on_the_ground.jpg#/media/File:Black_Friday,_attacked_suffragette_on_the_ground.jpg/

37. By People's History Museum - People's History Museum, Public domain, https://commons.wikimedia.org/w/index.php?curid=53343721/

38. Jacob Bright. Not credited. Public Domain, https://commons.wikimedia.org/w/index.php?curid=18286085/

39. By Unknown. http://thehistorybucket.blogspot.co.uk 1867) https://commons.wikimedia.org/wiki/File:Lilly_or_Lily_Maxwell_c.1867.jpg#/media/File:Lilly_or_Lily_Maxwell_c.1867.jpg/

40. By W.D.Almoyd -
https://commons.wikimedia.org/w/index.php?curid=4903332/ The
Union Makes Us Strong – TUC History Online (TUC Library
Collections, London Metropolitan University)
http://www.unionhistory.info/matchworkers/ContactSheet.php?
Where=MulHasMultiMedia+%3D+%27y%27+AND+exists%28Dc1Subject_tab+
where+Dc1Subject+contains+%27Match+Workers%27%29+AND+exists%28Tuc
Package_tab+where+TucPackage+contains+%27Match+Workers%27%29&Quer
yPage=%2Fmatchworkers%2Fmatchworkers.php&LimitPerPage=20

41. By Unknown. 1888-
https://commons.wikimedia.org/w/index.php?curid=68728518
https://www.retronews.fr/node/103580?utm_source=push_echo0604
18&utm_medium=lien_lire_la_suite&utm_campaign=la-greve-
victorieuse-des-matchgirls-anglaises/

42. Wake up John. Liberal poster. By Library of the London School
of Economics and Political Science (Ten Years of Toryism). No
restrictions, via Wikimedia Commons.
https://commons.wikimedia.org/wiki/File:Ten_Years_of_Toryism.jp
g#/media/File:Ten_Years_of_Toryism.jpg/

43. Picture of banner provided by Sally A. Barr

44. Picture of painting provided by Sally A. Barr

45. Picture provided by Sally A. Barr

SOURCES

Websites

1921 census data -
http://www.visionofbritain.org.uk/census/EW1921GEN/6/ Part V.—
Sexes, Ages and Marital Conditions. 1. Sexes. Retrieved August
2018.

BBC Archive-Lilian Lenton.
http://www.bbc.co.uk/archive/suffragettes/8322.shtml Retrieved July
2018.

Bob Osborn's A-to-Z of Yeovil's History -
http://www.yeovilhistory.info/ Retrieved June-August 2018

Brown, Lyn. Bow Match Women's Strike. Westminster Hall
Debates 8th October 2013.
https://www.theyworkforyou.com/whall/?id=2013-10-08c.22.1
Retrieved September 2018

Casey, Maurice J, 2018, "The Suffragettes Who Became
Communists", History Today (4 February)
www.historytoday.com/maurice-j-casey/suffragettes-who-became-
communists Retrieved August 2018

Cotswolds info. Wife Selling. https://www.cotswolds.info/strange-
things/wife-selling.shtml Retrieved September 2018.

Crawford, Elizabeth, "Suffrage Stories: 'From Frederick Street to
Winson Green': The Birmingham Women's Suffrage Campaign",
Woman and her Sphere (22 March2013)
https://tinyurl.com/ydboh28c Retrieved August 2018.

Department of the Official Report (Hansard), House of Lords,
Westminster (2 February 2000). "Lords Hansard text for 2 February
2000 (200202-03)". Publications.parliament.uk Retrieved August
2018

Fraser, Sir Hugh. "The Representation of the People Act, 1918 with explanatory notes". *Internet Archive.*
https://archive.org/details/representationof00frasrich Retrieved July 2018

Greater Manchester Lives. Manchester Society for Women's Suffrage.
http://gmlives.org.uk/results.html#imu[rid=ecatalogue.262930 Retrieved August 2018.

Hay, J. R. The Origins of the Liberal Welfare Reforms. Studies in Economic and Social History. Complete online. *http://history-books.weebly.com/uploads/6/9/9/0/6990231/liberal_welfare_reforms_jr_hay_1.pdf* Retrieved July 2018

History Extra. Website for BBC History Magazine and BBC world Histories Magazine.
https://www.historyextra.com/period/edwardian/cat-and-mouse-force-feeding-the-suffragettes/ Retrieved September 2018

Jackson, Sarah, 2015, "The Suffragettes Weren't Just White, Middle-class Women Throwing Stones", *Guardian* (12 October), www.theguardian.com/commentisfree/2015/oct/12/suffragettes-white-middle-class-women-pankhursts Retrieved July 2018

Law, Cheryl. (1997) Suffrage and Power: The Women's Movement 1918 – 1928. London, I B Tauris. Review by Dr Krista Cowman, University of York. **https://www.history.ac.uk/reviews/review/270** Retrieved: August 2018

Leigh Rayment's Peerage Page - Notes from House of Commons Constituencies for The Wolverhampton East by-election of 1908.
http://www.leighrayment.com/commons/Wcommons5.htm
Retrieved July -August 2018.

Mail Online – Southwest News Service and Chris Summers for Mailonline 29th January 2017. Pictured: First woman who EVER voted in Britain after electoral roll mix-up gave her the vote seven years before any other female.

http://www.dailymail.co.uk/news/article-4168786/Pictured-woman-voted-Britain.html#ixzz53thxqVlS . Retrieved 2018.

NUWSS Pamphlets - https://www.bl.uk/collection-items/nuwss-pamphlets/ Retrieved June 2018.

O'Callaghan, Bren. Our Father who art a Liberal. A daughter's mission. *http://www.bbc.co.uk/legacies/myths_legends/england/manchester/article_5.shtml Retrieved August 2018.*

Parliamentary Business. Appendix 1. 8.36. https://publications.parliament.uk/pa/cm199798/cmselect/cmhaff/768/768ap12.htm Retrieved September 2018

Purvis, June, Force-feeding of Hunger-striking Suffragettes, *Times Higher Education.* 26 April 1996. https://www.timeshighereducation.com/news/force-feeding-of-hunger-striking-suffragettes/93438.article Retrieved July 2018.

Rachael Attwood Hamard, Before you celebrate the centenary of women voting, remember that it isn't actually the triumph you think it is. Monday 5 February 2018. https://www.independent.co.uk/voices/100-years-centenary Retrieved August 2018.

Ridge. Sophie. Sky News Presenter. Sky Views: Who was the first British woman to vote? https://news.sky.com/story/sky-views-who-was-the-first-british-woman-to-vote-10808388/ Retrieved June 2018

Rix, Kathryn. .Before the vote was won: women in politics, 1832-68. Blog Post. Retrieved July 2018.

Sandhu, Serina. The court case that legally denied women the vote — and the women who voted anyway. February 2018. i news. The essential daily Briefing, https://inews.co.uk/news/uk/court-case-legally-denied-women-vote-women-voted-anyway/ Retrieved August 2018.

Schoonmaker, James 19th October 2014. The Suffragette Split. Manchester Historian. http://manchesterhistorian.com/2014/the-suffragette-split/ Retrieved August 2018

Surrey History Centre. Electoral Registers Guide. Electoral Registration and the Registers before 1918. https://www.surreycc.gov.uk/__data/assets/pdf_file/0016/36322/6-Electoral-registration-and-the-registers-before-1918.pdf Retrieved August 2018

The History of Wolverhampton. The City and its People. http://www.wolverhamptonhistory.org.uk/politics/women/suffragett es/index.html?sid=03ad4211f46444fabfbdb45761782629 Retrieved July 2018

The Telegraph. Women Voted 75 years before they were legally allowed to in 1918. https://www.telegraph.co.uk/women/womens-politics/9933592/Women-voted-75-years-before-they-were-legally-allowed-to-in-1918.html Retrieved August 2018

The Reform Act 1832 - https://www.parliament.uk/about/living-heritage/evolutionofparliament/houseofcommons/reformacts/overvie w/reformact1832/ Retrieved July 2018.

The University of Edinburgh. Our History http://ourhistory.is.ed.ac.uk/index.php/First_Graduation_of_Female_ Students,_1893 Retrieved August 2018

The Women's Library (London School of Economics). Franklin, Hugh (1889–1962); suffragist. Retrieved August 2018.

University of Glasgow https://www.universitystory.gla.ac.uk/women-background/ Retrieved August 2018.

Welfare reforms http://history-books.weebly.com/uploads/6/9/9/0/6990231/liberal_welfare_reform s_jr_hay_1.pdf Retrieved July 2018

Newspaper Articles

Aberdeen Press & Journal. Suffragist Scenes at Yeovil. Wednesday 1st December 1909. Page 6.

Berwickshire News and General Advertiser. A Woman Voter. Tuesday 30th January 1906. Page 7.

Birmingham Daily. Gazette. South Somerset Polling. The only woman voter supports Unionist Candidate. Wednesday 22nd November1911. Page 5.

Birmingham Daily Gazette. Suffragist Raid. Women fail to rush the House of Commons. 150 Arrests. Propaganda reinforced by window smashing. Wednesday 22nd November1911. Page 5.

Birmingham Daily Gazette. A by-election Telegram Wednesday 22nd November1911. Page 4.

Birmingham Daily Gazette. One woman one vote. Unity Dorking. Saturday 23rd November 1912. Page 6.

Buckingham Advertiser and North Bucks Free Press. Woman voter. Saturday 22nd January 1910. Page 8.

Common Cause. Keswick Liberal Club Votes for Women's Suffrage. Thursday 25th November 1909. Page 9.

Daily Mirror. Suffragettes storm the House. March the 21st 1907. Front Page

Daily Mirror. Violent scenes at Westminster. 19th of November 1910. Front page

Daily Mirror. South Somerset denounces the Servant Tax. 23rd of November 1911. Front Page

Daily Telegraph &Courier (London). Election Notes. Monday 22nd January 1906. Page 6. And the 25th January Page 10

Daily Telegraph &Courier (London). Wednesday 6th May 1908. Page 12.

Daily Telegraph & Courier (London). Somerset By-Election. Yesterday's Polling Wednesday 22nd November 1911. Page 11.

Dundee Courier. Most Women Think the Same. Friday, 26th September 1913. Page 8.

Dundee Evening Telegraph. Notice. Tuesday 25th January 1910. Page 4.

Evening Star. Another Woman Voter. Tuesday 9th October 1900. Page 3.

Exeter & Plymouth Gazette. A Woman Voting in a Parliamentary election. Tuesday 12th July 1887. Page 4.

Exeter & Plymouth Gazette. Our London Letter. House of Commons. Friday Night. Saturday 9th March 1907. Page 3.

Gloucester Citizen. Woman Voter refused. Tuesday 18th January 2010. Page 6.

Gloucestershire Echo, Polling at Wolverhampton. 5th of May 1908. Page 4.

Lancashire Evening Post. Wolverhampton Polling. Suffragist's Triumph with a Woman Voter. Tuesday 5th May 1908. Page 3.

Leeds Mercury. Disappointed Woman Voter 18th January 1906. Page 3.

Leeds Mercury. Woman discovered with a Vote. No intention to use it. 25th March 1909. Page 5.

Leicester Daily Post. The Census Form. Friday 17th March 1911. Page 4.

Leicester Daily Post. Mr Lloyd George on Woman Suffrage. Saturday 25th March 1911. Page 4.

London Daily News. Another Woman Voter. Thursday 11th October 1900. Page 3.

London Daily News. Still Another Woman Voter. Saturday 27th January 1906. Page 8.

London Daily News. Previous conflicts. 21st March 1907. Page 7.

London Daily News. Two women's names found on the voter's register. 29th March 1909. Page 7.

Manchester Courier and Lancashire General Advertiser. Preparations for the Election. Thursday, 4th October1883. *Page 8.*

Nottingham Journal. Another Woman Voter. Saturday 27th January 1906. Page 6.

Oxfordshire Weekly News. Woman Voter refused. Wednesday 26 January 1910. Page 8

Pall Mall Gazette. Only Woman Voter. Wednesday 27th November 1912. Page 3.

Portsmouth Evening News. More Lady Voters. Monday 22nd January 1906. Page 3.

Sheffield Evening Telegraph. Women as Parliamentary Electors. A Confusion of Christian Names. 24th August 1895. Page 4.

Sheffield Evening Telegraph. Woman voter cheered. Thursday 25th January 1906. Page 4.

Sheffield Evening Telegraph. A Woman's Triumph. Allowed to record a vote. 5th May 1908. Page 5.

Shepton Mallet Journal. Woman Voter refused. Friday 21st of January 1910. Page 3.

Sunderland Daily Echo and Shipping Gazette. A Woman Voter, Saturday 15th January 1910.Page 5.

Taunton Courier and Western Advertiser. A Lady Voter. Wednesday 17th January 1906. Page 1.

Taunton Courier and Western Advertiser. South Somerset Election. Woman Voter at Yeovil.

Wednesday 29th November 1911. Page 3.

The Conservative and Unionist Women's Franchise Review. General Information. Monday 1st August.1910-Page 41

The Globe. Wolverhampton fight. Polling day. Woman Records her vote. Tuesday 5th May.1908. Page 7.

The Gloucester Journal. The Militant Suffragists'. 2nd August. 1913. Page 10.

The Irish Times. Wolverhampton by-election. Female records a Vote. 6th May 1908. Page 5.

The Liverpool Mercury. Is Mary Boddy 'a lady?' Thursday 16th September 1868. Page 8.

The Liverpool Mercury. London Notes. Saturday 26th September 1868. Page 5.

The Liverpool Mercury. The Right of Women to Vote. Tuesday 10th November 1868. Page 9.

The Liverpool Mercury. Day to Day in Liverpool. Wednesday 26th September 1900. Page 9.

The Sketch. Small Talk of the Week. Wednesday, 24th January 1906. Page 7.

Votes for Women. Wolverhampton. Thursday 7th May 1908. Page 138.

Western Chronicle. Somerset Appeal Tribunal. Yeovil & District Cases. *Friday 11th 1916. Page 6.*

Western Chronicle. What our boys are doing. Yeovil. 31st August 1917. Page 6.

Western Daily Press. A Woman Voter in Dorset. Saturday 27th January 1906. Page 12.

Western Gazette. Women's Suffrage. Friday, 16th March 1883. Page 6.

Western Gazette. The by-election. West Somerset. Suffragette Support for the Unionist. Friday 14th July 1911. Page 12

Western Gazette. Woman in Court. Friday the 25th August 1911.

Western Gazette. The Unionist Campaign. Friday 17th November.1911. Page 3.

Western Gazette. South Somerset Election. Woman Voter Yeovil 24th November 1911. Page 5

Women's Franchise. Current topics. Leicester Women's Suffrage Society. September 7th 1907. Pages 128-129

Women's Franchise. Through the Thorny Way at Wolverhampton. Thursday 14th May 1908. Page 6.

Women's Franchise. Working Woman and the Vote. 2nd September 1909. Page 751

Women's Freedom League. Through the thorny way at Wolverhampton. Thursday 14th May 1908. Page 542.

Yorkshire Post & Leeds Intelligencer. Incidents of the Polling. Wednesday 6th May. Page 7.

Bibliography

Craig. F.W.S. (1989) British Electoral Facts 1832–1987, 5th edition. Aldershot Hants, England. Parliamentary Research Services 1989.

Crawford, Elizabeth. (1999) The Women's Suffrage Movement: A Reference Guide 1866-1928. Routledge.

Foot, Paul. (2005) The Vote: How it was Won and How it was Undermined. Penguin.

Gleadle, K. & Richardson S. (Editors.). (2000) Women in British Politics 1760-1860: The Power of the Petticoat. Palgrave Macmillan UK.

Harris, Bernard. (2004) The Origins of the British Welfare State: Social Welfare in England and Wales, 1800–1945. Palgrave. 2004 Edition.

Hunt, Cathy. (2014) The National Federation of Women Workers, *1906-1921.* Palgrave.

Jackson, Sarah, and Taylor, Rosemary (2014) Voices from History: East London Suffragettes: History Press. e-book version.

Lee, Geoffrey, (2008) The People's Budget: An Edwardian Tragedy. Shepheard- Walwyn (Publishers) Ltd. 2nd Edition.

Lennox, Geraldine (1932) The Suffragette Spirit. Volume 4 of Suffragette Lectures. Suffragette Fellowship 1932.

Liddington, Jill. (2014) Vanishing for the Vote: Suffrage, Citizenship and the Battle for the Census. Manchester University Press.

Murray, Bruce K. (1980) The People's Budget, 1909-1910: Lloyd George and Liberal Politics. Oxford University Press.

Rosen, Andrew, (2013) Rise Up, Women! The Militant Campaign of the Women's Social and Political Union. 1903-1914. Volume. 32. Routledge Library Editions: Women's History.

AUTHORS' NOTE

As all proceeds from this book will be used to help the One Million Project with publication and promotion costs for their creative projects, pictures used were taken from those listed in the public domain. While every effort was made to accurately record sources and the content in this book, errors can occur. The author's will make any required changes on request and include these in future editions.

A newspaper report in November 1911 stated that Frances was a widow. There is some evidence, however, to suggest that her husband, Edward, was still alive at this time. In the census completed in April of that same year, Frances lists herself as married—despite the option available to list herself as a widow. Also, on Frances's death certificate in 1917, it states 'Wife of Edward Connelly, Hotel Manager.' Frances and Edward could have been living apart. If Edward was indeed managing a hotel, this could account for the difficulty in tracing his whereabouts after 1901.

ACKNOWLEDGEMENTSs

Thanks to Bob Osborn for his permission to use pictures from his amazing resource; A-to-Z of Yeovil's History - http://www.yeovilhistory.info/

Thanks to NeoLeaf Press for support in publishing and promoting this book.

Steven J Pemberton, Michael Walsh, Kate Stewart, Sherry Logsdon and Douglas Debelak, thank you for reading and commenting on early drafts.

Thanks to Jason Greenfield, CEO of the One Million Project, for bringing Frances Connelly's story to the attention of the OMP members and for commissioning this book.

To all of the One Million Project members, a huge thankyou for giving your time and creative talents to help raise funds towards cradicating homelessness and for cancer research.

Links to the One Million Project Anthologies

myBook.to/OMPFiction

myBook.to/OMPThriller

myBook.to/OMPFantasy

mybook.to/OMPVarietyAnthology

Thanks for reading. If you enjoyed this book, please consider leaving an honest review.

10840571R00088

Printed in Great Britain
by Amazon